MW00711191

Before I
Heart Away

A practical guide to understanding how the lack of a positive father figure in childhood impacts all of a daughter's relationships later in life, especially with men, and greatly distorts the view of the heavenly Father.

Contributors:
Judith Ames David, Editor
Linda M. Smith
Dr. Wayne Shaw

www.TotalPublishingAndMedia.com

Before You Give Your Heart Away
Copyright © 2011 by Judith Ames David. All rights reserved.

ISBN: 978-1-936750-28-3

Acknowledgements

L ife is a journey and so is a book. In the beginning stages, compiling *Before You Give Your Heart Away* was like putting together a puzzle. In this case, though, it seemed like the pieces were scattered all over the house, and there was no picture on the top of the box. I knew that God wanted me to write about my experiences concerning the lack of a relationship with my earthly father, as well as my heavenly Father, but it greatly lacked focus.

My pastor, Dr. Wayne Shaw, gave me numerous books to read, and I did a great deal of research on my own. He was also instrumental in checking the accuracy of theological issues every step of the way. When I wanted personal testimony, I asked a woman I knew had a great story to tell. As I asked her to tell her story, another woman offered to give hers as well. Anna Shaw, director of the Christian H.E.L.P. Center, told me about Linda Smith, director of the Abundant Blessings Center, and her powerful testimony. Then I asked Dr. Shaw to write the last part. Over a year passed during the research phase. Just as I was getting discouraged about the project, all the personal testimonies started coming in. Then eventually the other parts of the book fell into place.

Until a few years ago, I wasn't sure what a father was supposed to do. During this project, my heavenly Father encouraged me when I was ready to give up, guided me to the right people at the right time, and inspired me to write. After all, isn't that what fathers do? My task was to trust my heavenly Father to see me through. To Him, I am the most grateful for this and for all things.

I especially want to thank all the contributors named and anonymous who gave of their time and selves. I also appreciate all those who wrote endorsements and Teresa Raymond for writing the foreword, as well as all those who read and reviewed the book in all stages of the process. Thanks to all my friends and family who encouraged and supported me, especially my husband Arley.

This book is dedicated to

all the fathers who get up every day

to be the best fathers they can be,

knowing that the only perfect father

is our heavenly Father.

What People Are Saying

I have two daughters still in the home. When the older daughter in middle school walks out the door, I always make sure that she dresses modestly, knowing what most young boys have on their minds. With sex dominating TV and the news, sometimes it falls on deaf ears. With *Before You Give Your Heart Away,* I now have a book all the family can read and discuss. I am also considering using it as a springboard for discussion in my Sunday school class for college age students.
Bob Edmondson
Finish Carpenter

As a middle school nurse, I wish I could get the female students to read a book like this before they make the mistake of being sexually active at such an early age. Some have already made that mistake, but I believe that God's love can give them the strength to wait for a committed relationship in marriage later on. Young boys also need to understand that a girl is more than a sex toy, and that getting a girl pregnant at a young age will affect him the rest of his life.
Janet Edmondson
Middle School Nurse

I salute those who have contributed to *Before You Give Your Heart* Away with such humility and honesty. May the reader have ears to hear and eyes to see.
Nancy Edwards
Peer Counselor/Abundant Blessings Center
Delaware County Jail Ministry

As a grandparent, I feel that the information in this book will be helpful to many women by learning from the mistakes of others. Many years ago, I worked at a hospital that housed a home for unwed mothers. At birth the babies were given up for adoption. Being a single mom back then was considered a disgrace. Because abortion was illegal, a woman took a big risk by having an illegal one, usually by an unprofessional and/or unscrupulous person. Many women died, which left their families to live with the loss of an infant and a loved one. In today's world, there are more choices. Abortions are legal and relatively safe, but young women often live a lifetime of regret after choosing this option. This book shows young women a better way to avoid the pitfalls of an unwanted pregnancy

Ann Loewe, R.N.

Before You Give Your Heart Away is a great resource for sharing with women of any age the importance of guarding your heart. It contains a two-fold blessing, combining the truth and healing of God's Word with relevant real life stories. It is a message that every young woman needs to hear!

Thomas Hawkins
Youth Pastor

The book reads like an interesting story but doubles as a guide to learning the way to cope with problems. The questions at the end of each chapter and each of the four parts are thought provoking and when answered honestly, will lead to new insights, healing, and trust in God. I have read many stories and psychological solutions to the problems that are faced by not living with a positive father figure, but I have never seen so much scripture and experience of those who have looked to God for the solution to their problems. I am torn between wanting to keep the book for myself and giving it to someone else to learn from. Thank you all for writing the book. I am grateful that there are people who are willing to share their life stories and the way God helped them live a fruitful and victorious life.

Nancy Dooley
Retired Educator

Being the father of two sons and no daughters, I was somewhat surprised when I was given a copy of a book about father/daughter relationships to read. I was puzzled wondering what a book like this had to do with me. *Before You Give Your Heart Away* captivated my heart as I read it, not only causing me to examine relationships with my wife, sons, and deceased earthly father, but, most of all, it illuminated the love of my heavenly Father. It clarified my understanding of my past relationships, as well as challenged me to demonstrate our heavenly Father's love in current and future encounters. *Before You Give Your Heart Away* has much to offer both women and men—young and old.

Joe Nowlin
Rivers of Life Ministries

I have done a great deal of counseling with people who have issues with substance abuse, mentally ill patients, and prisoners. The premise on which you base this book—mainly the father/daughter relationship—has a lot of merit. It does seem that women who do not have a good father figure do not know what to look for in a relationship. Many of their problems stem from this original relationship with their father. I would recommend this book especially to those who have problems with substance abuse. Actually, anyone can, but I find that this is a bigger problem with those who are addicted. Also, the scriptural references and the relationship with God reminders will help people who are in AA. Their whole program is based on their relationship with God or higher power.

Sister Angela Houska ASC

Getting the Most from This Book

Before You Give Your Heart Away is divided into four parts. Part One, "Earthly Father/Heavenly Father" deals with information and testimony about the importance of the father/daughter relationship, as well as how the lack of an appropriate father figure distorts the view of the heavenly Father. Part Two, "Hiding the Shame," emphasizes how a child can take on the shame of what someone else has done to them. It also contains personal testimonies about forgiving others, forgiving one's self, and finding a closer walk with God. In Part Three, Linda Smith's powerful story shows how heartache and regret can be turned into learning life's lessons, personal growth, and passing comfort and wisdom to the next generation. In Part Four, "Moving Forward God's Way," Dr. Wayne Shaw discusses personal experiences in his ministry in working with people who were a product of poor parenting. He also shows hope for the future by encouraging us to allow our heavenly Father to guide us through life. Each of the four parts builds one upon the other to a journey of understanding.

"Questions to Consider" are at the close of each chapter. "Going Deeper" and "Responding to Scripture" conclude each of the four parts.

"Questions to Consider" merely brings out the main points in each chapter as a reading and comprehension check for individual reflection or group discussion.

"Going Deeper" are personal questions geared toward the experiences of each individual. All may not apply. In a group setting, these more in-depth questions should not only bring a deeper understanding of self to each individual but also give each participant a chance to learn and grow through the interaction of all the members of the group.

"Responding to Scripture" demonstrates that the Bible is, indeed, applicable to issues in today's world. Each scripture relates to what was discussed in that particular part. For example, in Part One we wanted to emphasize the enormity of God's love, the constancy of God's love, and learning to trust our heavenly Father with all cares and concerns.

A suggested reading list appears at the back of the book. Besides the Bible, they are books we learned from that changed our lives in some way.

Before You Give Your Heart Away is not just a book to be read quickly and put aside. It should be used in an individual or group setting as a journey to personal growth and healing.

Pass on the Love! (and the book)

To: _____

In Honor of: _____

By: _____

Date: _____

Message: _____

_____

_____

_____

_____

_____

Pass on to family members, church libraries, church groups, pregnancy centers, domestic violence centers, prison ministries, recovery groups, etc.

Contents

Foreword

Judith David was motivated to compile *Before You Give Your Heart Away* for personal reasons. As a young adult, she would hear people say that God is our heavenly Father. In her mind she would think, "No, thank you. I don't need another father." In this book she shares her journey of discovery, a journey where she learns that God is the loving Father she never knew growing up and did not believe existed. The heavenly Father, even in the compiling of the book, healed her heart from years of hurt, taught her to see herself as the cherished creation that He sees her, and gave her the ability to have healthy relationships. Judith's experience uniquely equips her to speak to others who have traveled the same path.

The theme of loss, redemption, blessing, and wholeness through Christ can been seen in the stories of the other contributors as well. They all opened their hearts and told their stories in order that others may learn from their experiences and understand the need for a heavenly Father, even if an earthly father was not available. All were truly changed by the love of the Father God. *Before You Give Your Heart Away* combines psychological concepts, biblical knowledge, and insights into real life experiences that will resonate with today's young women.

Teresa Raymond
B.S. in Business & Organizational Leadership
Millikin University
Decatur, Illinois
Magna Cum Laude
Class of 2007

Before You Give Your Heart Away

H ow do you choose who you want to date or who you will marry? I'm sure you have certain criteria, such as looks, intelligence, personality, and a sense of humor. Of course, there's that certain chemistry that everyone talks about. If you have had bad marriages or a string of unhealthy relationships, is there some reason for that pattern? Do you seem to choose the same type of man over and over again? Could there be some subconscious factors in how you choose a man with whom to have a relationship? Psychologists think there are.

Young women who grow up in a home where their father is loving, provides for them, gives them time and attention, and treats them with respect will most likely form more healthy emotional bonds with other men than those who were abused, neglected, or physically and emotionally abandoned. A young woman whose "love tank" has not been filled by her parents often ends up in a relationship with a young man whose "love tank" has not been filled by his parents.[1] When one party is not able to meet the emotional needs of the other, it usually ends in heartache, resulting in one bad relationship after another. This dysfunction will continue into future generations until some kind of intervention occurs like professional counseling.

In this book, four women tell their stories of challenging childhood experiences, broken relationships, breaking the cycle of family dysfunction, and healing by moving forward God's way. Reliving these experiences were painful, in most cases, but all said that if it helped only one person not go through what they did, it would be worth it. In addition, it is our hope that you who have taken the wrong road will find your way home through self-discovery and a spiritual awakening, allowing God to heal your hurts and letting Him be your guide in the journey of life.

This book isn't about male bashing. Authorities on the subject believe that teenage pregnancy, drug use, and promiscuity have a root in the failure to attach to a father figure. These stories tell of fathers who are emotionally unavailable and/or abusive in some way, but some fathers fail to be effective for reasons beyond their control. With the high divorce rate, some fathers are unable to spend as much time with their children as they wish when they are not the custodial parent. Some fathers suffer long illnesses or may have to be absent because of military duty. During times of economic hardship, fathers often have to work more than one job to keep the family going.

A mother's role is extremely important, and young men need an adequate male role model also, but this book will focus only on the father/daughter relationship. This book isn't about blaming your parents for all your problems either. The ladies who tell their stories are overcomers and used their faith in God to heal. I have a Master's degree in counseling, have read a boat load of psychology and self-help books, and have improved the quality of my life and my relationships to a great extent over the years since my youth. But until I let God be in the role of my heavenly Father in later years, I was never truly healed and at peace with myself. It was a long, hard journey but definitely worth the effort.

Before You Give Your Heart Away is not to take the place of professional counseling if the problem is deep seated or has a physical or addictive component. Instead, it should be just a starting place for you to become more aware of the factors involved in choosing a mate for life, remembering that you are not just choosing a husband, but the father of your future children.

For other women, you may be divorced and would like to experience healthier relationships in the future. Perhaps, you may just want to be more at peace with yourself and explore whether or not it is necessary to have a man in your life to be happy. Another important issue discussed is how your view of your earthly father greatly impacts your view of the heavenly Father.

We all contributed to this book in hopes that we could spare you some of the pain we experienced, full well knowing that everyone has to make their own mistakes and take their own journey through life. We also have the hope that you will find forgiveness, healing, and wholeness in your life. We are from your grandparents' generation, in most cases. Unlike when we were growing up, there is more knowledge about family dysfunction and are more resources available to help. Also, the stigma of admitting problems and seeking counseling is much less than it was in the past. We all discovered that we had to find other appropriate male role models to fill the emptiness of not having a healthy relationship with our own fathers. I don't believe that God can totally take the place of a father, but as my pastor says, He can "fill in the gaps." And God does send us others to show His love and heal our hurts.

In the final part, a pastor, who has done extensive family counseling, has had over twenty foster children in his home he and his wife have cared for, and has been in the ministry for over forty years, offers the male point of view concerning effective parenting. He also tells the story of God's love and how it applies to you and your life. We present this book to you with our love and prayers.

Judith David
Editor and Contributor

Part One
Earthly Father/Heavenly Father

by

Judith David

Chapter 1
Earthly Father/Heavenly Father

What does a good father look like? He makes his children a top priority. He lets them know verbally and nonverbally how important they are to him and how much they are loved. No one has the perfect father because we are all human. A father doesn't have to be perfect; he just needs to be involved in the lives of his children. The involved father spends time with his children.

Rick Warren, author, pastor, and counselor, describes the importance of spending time with your children in this way: "The essence of love is not what we think or do or provide for others, but how much we give *of ourselves*. Men, in particular, often don't understand this. Many have said to me, 'I don't understand my wife and kids. I provide everything they need. What more could they want?' They want you. Your eyes, your ears, your time, your attention, your presence, your focus—your time. Nothing can take the place of that."[1]

Back in our parents' and grandparents' generation, we thought that a man should be concerned mostly with working and providing for the family financially and be there to support the mother whenever needed. Today, we know that a father's role is much more important than that, especially in forming his daughter's sexual identity. "Little girls develop their femininity in contrast to the father's masculinity." When that normal interaction fails to occur, the emotions become warped.[2]

If the relationship is healthy, the father is his young daughter's first love.[3] Through him, she learns how men should treat women and how women should treat men.[4] When a girl grows up, the father/daughter experience still affects her in all she does—sometimes in ways she doesn't understand.[5]

If the daughter doesn't receive enough love and attention from a father in her childhood, she will carry the pain for the rest of her life. It will affect her relationship with her spouse, her children, and everyone else. This unresolved pain from the past will cause emotional havoc in all future relationships.[6]

Very young children believe that their parents are always right. When they are old enough to realize that problems do exist in their family, they tend to blame themselves. If children cannot identify any specific misbehavior that may have caused their parents to withhold love and comfort, the next step is to assume that they must be bad in general.[7]

In Robert McGee's book, *Father Hunger*, he says, "We don't just want our fathers to love us, we need them to love us. This emotional hunger acts in many ways like physical hunger. If we aren't provided with what is the best for us, we will soon seek other, less healthy substitutes."[8]

Some young girls turn to other men in search of acceptance about the time they reach dating age. Others avoid intimate relationships altogether, vowing never to let any man hurt them as their father did. As adults, these women who have never received a proper role model from a father will pass on the pain and emptiness to the next generation.

Our relationship with our earthy father affects our view of our heavenly Father. "Those who are loved and affirmed by their parents tend to have a fairly healthy self-concept, and usually find it easy to believe that God is a loving God. Those whose parents have been neglectful, manipulative, or condemning usually feel that they have to earn a sense of worth, and that God is aloof, demanding, and/or cruel."[9]

God is our Creator, Lord and Master, Judge, Redeemer, Father, Savior, and much more.[10] But as children of dysfunctional families, we have difficulty knowing what role God plays in our lives because we don't fully understand all the roles our earthly fathers were supposed to play. Our fathers may have been inconsistent in their moods, personalities, and discipline. Perhaps, they were uncaring, neglectful, or abusive in their parenting. Because of this, it is difficult for us to grasp God's nature.

In Tim Sledge's book, *Making Peace With Your Past,* he uses the following illustration from Mark Twain's "Old Times on the Mississippi" to explain the unchanging nature of God:

> "Mark Twain told of a lecture he had received from a Mississippi River ship's captain. The captain told his apprentice that the river might appear different under different kinds of moonlight. He said that on a clear night heavy shadows would hide obstacles, and on pitch-dark nights all the shores would seem to be straight. On nights of gray the shores would have no shape. Twain objected, 'Oh, don't say any more, please! Have I got to learn the shape of the river according to all these five hundred thousand different ways?' The captain responded, 'No! You only learn the shape of the river; and you learn it with such absolute certainty that you can always steer by the shape that's in your head, and never mind the one that's before your eyes.' "[11]

Our earthly father might have been inconsistent with his love, discipline, and moods, but our heavenly Father never changes. Because of this, we must learn to focus on God's unchanging nature. "Regardless of circumstances, and how you feel, hang on to God's unchanging character. Remind yourself what you know to be eternally true about God. He is good, he loves me, he is with me, he knows what I'm going through, and he has a good plan for my life."[12]

The lack of love and attention from our earthly father left a void in our hearts. Because of this, it is hard for us to comprehend the enormity of God's love:

"For I am convinced that neither death nor life, neither angels nor demons, neither the present nor the future, nor any powers, neither height nor depth, nor anything else in all creation, will be able to separate us from the love of God that is in Christ Jesus our Lord." (Romans 8:38-39)

Questions to Consider

(1) What does a good father do to show his love for his children?

(2) Why are fathers so important in a daughter's healthy development into adulthood?

(3) What happens when a daughter fails to receive enough love from her father?

(4) How does this affect her future relationships? Why?

(5) Why do some young women turn to men in search of acceptance when they reach dating age?

(6) How can some young women who have never experienced a proper male role model pass on the pain to her own children?

(7) How does a daughter's relationship with her earthly father affect her relationship with the heavenly Father? Why?

(8) What roles should an earthly father play?

(9) What roles does your heavenly Father play?

(10) Why would it be hard for a child who has been abused or neglected to understand how much God loves us?

(11) How can we learn to trust and love our heavenly Father? Will it happen overnight or will it be a process? Explain.

Chapter 2

I Once Was Lost

In the autumn of the year and the autumn of my life, I look out the window and see white pelicans near the island on the Elk River arm of Grand Lake in Grove, Oklahoma. In early October in the Midwest, the leaves are just now beginning to turn colors. In some years, the leaves are scorched from the searing summer heat and never turn a vibrant array of colors before they fall. Just like the leaves, there were times when I wondered if I would find beauty in my life before I died.

It's 4:00, and I'll have time to watch *Oprah* for a while before I start cooking supper for my husband Arley and me. Today's show deals with the subject of bipolar disorder. A man named Chris comments about how his illness has affected his family. "The disease has affected everything—social life, married life. Friendships are gone. I can't hold a job down," he says with despair. "Living with bipolar disorder is like a train wreck." During some of his episodes, he reports to have thrown a television down the stairs, punched holes in the wall, broken expensive furniture, and kicked in the fenders of his car after it got stuck in the mud. "I'm not allowed to be alone with my kids because they think I'm going to hurt them and I won't know it."

Oprah asks his wife what the children say during these rages. She says something to the effect that they say, "Daddy is having another episode." She worries that his behavior is affecting their children.[13]

Saying this transports me back over fifty years to my childhood, growing up with a father who was prone to rages. He died when he was sixty from a third heart attack. He was a locomotive engineer on the M-K-T or Katy railroad in Parsons, Kansas. After the first two, the doctor just placed him in the hospital for a week or two until he was feeling better. He died in 1970, and bypass surgery wouldn't be a common procedure for several years. Another phenomenon that wasn't treated or widely recognized much back in those days was bipolar disorder. As time passed and knowledge of this disorder came to light, I was convinced that he definitely fit the pattern.

I was never physically abused—thank God! Usually the rages weren't directed toward me, but just living to witness those rages affected my life in a profound way. He had what they called back in those days, "nervous breakdowns." Again, he was sent to the hospital, came back, and the cycle would repeat itself.

Does it affect children? Yes! From my own experience, I can tell you that it affected my life in many ways. I feel that I was emotionally stunted as a child. It was difficult, if not impossible, for me to process my feelings with anyone. I was never taught to do this. The family was so focused on not getting my father upset that it never occurred to me that I could express how I felt about anything. When children block out negative emotions to protect themselves from being hurt, they tend to block out positive emotions as well. People who have experienced emotional or physical trauma in their early years often can't remember large portions of their childhood, even the good things. I never learned to trust—especially men. I was afraid to approach my father, even when he was in a good mood because I never knew when his mood would change. I was a little girl, and he was a very large man over six feet tall.

My mother and I were very close. She treated me more like an equal than a child. We would discuss what was going on, and she would explain that Dad had been mistreated as a child. Dad would work passenger trains and would be gone weeks at a time. While he was gone, we had a ball. She took us to church and taught us good values, and she was somewhat of a kid herself. We had a very old house, and she had the attitude that we couldn't hurt it much anyway. All three of us kids loved her and minded her mostly because we didn't want to hurt her. Like most kids, we pushed her to the limit at times, but when she got mad, we usually got her laughing.

When Dad came home, the whole mood of the house changed. We "walked on egg shells" for fear he would blow up. I know that most fathers are usually stricter, which he was. The problem was that he was never consistent. Sometimes we could do almost anything, and at other times he would rage over the smallest things. I can remember him saying in anger, "It wasn't my idea to have children. It was your mother's." He threatened suicide so many times that we somewhat got used to it. Not that anyone can ever get used to it, but I had to tuck it away in the recesses of my mind to keep me sane. As a matter of fact, I tucked most of my emotions away to the point that I grew up not knowing how I felt at times. To avoid the hurt, I became emotionally numb.

He would rage over something trivial, and then the next day, we were expected to act like nothing had happened the day before. We were living a lie. Like most children back in the fifties, we were always told to be on our best behavior when we were out in public. When I would visit friends, I just assumed that their father was just like mine, even though they treated me with kindness. I just reasoned that they would turn into a different person like my dad often did when no one else was around.

I went to church most of my childhood at Central Avenue Christian Church in Parsons, Kansas. When I was twelve, Mom switched to the Episcopal church so that Dad would go to church with us. In church I would often hear the minister say, "God is our heavenly Father, just like your earthly father." My thoughts would always be, "Who needs another one of those?" Back in those days, I had never heard of a personal relationship with God. I didn't know I was supposed to have one.

I went to a community college in Parsons for the first two years. When I left for college at Kansas State College in Pittsburg, Kansas, now called Pittsburg State University, I left my faith behind. I'm not blaming anyone for leaving my faith; it was my choice. All these years later, though, I do believe that I had trouble relating to my heavenly Father because my earthly father was angry and emotionally unavailable. I never remember having a real conversation with him.

My father couldn't help having bipolar disorder. They didn't have the understanding of the disease or medications like they have today. There were also other factors that kept him from living a normal life. Mom said that when he was five years old, he was dragged kicking and screaming from his mother. After their divorce, his dad got custody, just to get revenge on his mother. His father really didn't want him either, and so he was raised by an aunt. Because of his upbringing, he never learned to give and receive love. Even when we kids would tell him that we loved him, he wouldn't believe it.

I remember one day my grandmother Julia knocked on our door and told my mother that she had come there to die. This surprised all of us. She had never acted lovingly toward my father, and my mother really resented it. In spite of this, my mother even changed her diapers and took care of her until the very end. Mom told me later that Dad would sit and talk to her and hold her hand. I'm glad that there was some reconciliation before she died. My mother had unconditional love for people. As I look back, if it weren't for her, I don't know what path my life would have taken.

My father died instantly of a massive heart attack at the age of sixty. I was only twenty-four when he died. Mom said that he was ready to go to work and had sat down for a while to read an Episcopal prayer book in his final moments. I am sixty-five and just now starting to find many answers in my life. At that time, I didn't realize that I not only would have to grieve the loss of a father at an early age but also the loss of a father/daughter relationship that never had time to grow and mature. It took me years to understand the impact of this loss, to go through the healing process, and to let God be in the role of my heavenly Father.

Questions to Consider

(1)   How do the lives of children change when a parent suffers from a mental illness or an addiction?

(2)   How did the mood of the house change when Judith's father came home?

(3)   How much do negative comments from a parent affect the self-worth of a child?

(4)   Why do children hide the fact that things aren't normal at home? Do you think that these children get a warped view of what normal is?

(5)   Even though Judith had a very loving mother, can a mother's love completely take the place of a father's love? Why or why not?

(6)   Why do people who are hurt on a consistent basis become emotionally numb?

(7)   When children block out pain, what else do they block out?

(8)   Why did Judith have so much trouble comparing her earthly father to her heavenly Father?

(9)   What is unconditional love? How does it help provide a child with positive self-worth?

(10) Why is it important to recognize the pain of a lost relationship? Why is it important to go though the grief process?

Chapter 3
Our Father

A fter my mother's death in 2000 from the complications of Alzheimer's disease, I wrote a book called *Set Me Adrift in the Sea of Faith,* about how her struggle brought me back to church after a thirty-four year absence. During this time, I started attending a Christian writers group in Vinita, Oklahoma, for a short while. The leader Lavon asked us to write a devotional using a sound from our childhood. I could think of so many good sounds associated with my mother—the sound of her voice, popcorn cooking on the stove, and especially the sound of her laughter. I decided that since I had written an entire book about my mother's influence on my life and spirituality, I would write this devotional about my father. I struggled all one day and couldn't come up with anything positive to write about. My husband Arley asked what was wrong with me because I seemed so distant. It was then that I realized that the grief I felt was that of a lost relationship. It is important to recognize our losses in order to go through the mourning process so that we can move on to a happier and more fulfilled life.

Since I was in my early twenties when my father died, I didn't have a chance to know him as an adult. Over the years, I started remembering good things about him. I remembered him attending my dance recitals, teaching me my multiplication tables, and giving his whole paycheck to us to provide for our needs. Still, I missed out on having a real relationship with him. I reasoned that maybe part of the reason I had trouble relating to my heavenly Father was that I had never formed a loving attachment to my earthly father. The devotional called "Our Father" follows:

Even today the sound of a train's engine and the blare of the whistle takes me back over fifty years to the MKT railroad yards in Parsons, Kansas. Mom and we three kids would wait by the caller's office for Dad to get home from his run. The big black steam engine would break the silence of the night with the chug, puff, hiss, and clatter in a syncopated rhythm of power and urgency. My dad's large frame would disappear from the engineer's high perch, and he would lumber down the steps in bib overalls with his black metal lunch box in hand.

As time went by, Dad grew older and I grew up. On hot summer nights with the windows wide open, I would lie in bed and hear the distant lonely sound of a train whistle in the railroad yard grow louder and louder and then fade into the distance. Later on, Mom told me of Dad's depression, the "breakdowns," and the time she had to walk him part way to work to give him the courage to go. But he always went and provided well for us.

Often his angry voice would pierce the silence of the house and make me run and hide like the scared little rabbit that I was. He died before I had a chance to know him on equal terms as an adult. So many questions would never find an answer. Even now, when I hear the lonely whistle of a train passing in the night, I feel the sadness and regret of a relationship that was cut short by time and never allowed to grow to maturity.

Sometimes we feel that some family member or other significant person in our life has failed us. Sometimes we feel that we have failed them in some way. Our heavenly Father will never fail us. He does not come into our lives, make a lot of noise, and then fade into the distance. He knew us by name before we were born. He has counted every tear. He sent His son to die for our sins. He prepares a place for us to dwell with Him forever. According to 2 Corinthians 5:17, "Therefore, if anyone is in Christ, he is a new creation; the old has gone, the new has come!" With spiritual rebirth, the older order of things passes away when we let Christ into our hearts. In 1 Peter 5:7, we are told, "Cast all your anxiety on Him because He cares for you."

O Lord, help me to silence the angry voices of the past. When no one else seems to be there for me, let me remember to turn to You for the encouragement I need. Let me be what I seek to find in others. May I continue to grow by trusting and loving You. May I learn to relax in Your arms, my heavenly Father.

Questions to Consider

(1) As a adult, how does Judith look back to her childhood and explain her feelings about her father?

(2) Why did she describe herself as a "scared little rabbit"? How would that affect her feelings of self-worth?

(3) How important do you think it was that Judith's mother honestly explained her father's mental illness to her? Do you think that children tend to blame themselves when a parent is unhappy?

(4) Why has Judith had problems "silencing the angry voices of the past"?

(5) Why does she ask her heavenly Father to help her?

(6) Does her lack of trust in people and herself make it difficult for her to relax? Explain.

Chapter 4

Running from the Past

After graduating from college, I got out of Parsons as soon as I could to get away from the misery at home. I really loved my mother, but I longed for a life where I would be in control of my own destiny. I thought that it would be easy to create the life I wanted, not realizing that my childhood would continue to haunt me for many years to come. I had just completed school in Los Angeles to be a flight attendant for Continental Airlines. My first husband Rob, now deceased, and I met in college, and he had just landed a job with Continental Oil in Houston after completing his Master's degree. I put in a bid for Houston as my home base and got it.

A few months passed when I got a call from my mother that Dad was in the hospital after his second heart attack. By now, I was twenty-three. All three of us kids had been out of the house for a few years. I will never forget what happened when I went home to see him. Like I said, there had never been any meaningful conversation between my dad and myself. Mom and I would talk back and forth while Dad would throw in an occasional comment. He didn't seem very excited that I had flown back to see him.

When I turned to leave, he pleaded, "Judy, don't leave me." I had never heard him say anything like that or even that he loved me. I was so surprised and shocked I didn't know what to do or say. Those words haunted me the rest of my life. Rob and I were getting married in a few months. I had to get back to my job and my future husband. Subconsciously, I wanted to avoid the pain. I wanted to leave the past in the past. I had started a new life. Why did he want to make contact now?

Understanding my dilemma and my need to hurry to catch the plane back, Mom just said, "Richard," in somewhat of a scolding voice. I went back to hug him one more time, turned around, and just kept walking. I felt no attachment, just the guilt of leaving. This could have been the beginning of a relationship at that point. I could have at least called and asked to talk to him on the phone from time to time. After I went back to Houston, I would call Mom and ask how Dad was. Now, I realize how odd it was that I never asked to talk to him directly, nor he to me. I always just talked **through** Mom. Now that I look back, I walked out on my earthly father, just as I had walked out on my heavenly Father.

Questions to Consider

(1) When a child leaves home, can she truly leave her past behind?

(2) Why do you think that Judith was confused when her father said, "Don't leave me"?

(3) Why didn't she immediately start working on a better relationship when she had the opportunity? Did she know how?

(4) Why did she feel guilty when she had to leave to go back to her own life?

(5) Why did she continue to talk to her mother **about** her father, instead of talking to him directly?

Chapter 5

A Gift from My Heavenly Father

In the devotional I wrote called "Our Father," I realized that I had to grieve a relationship with a father who was angry and emotionally unavailable because of bipolar disorder and dysfunction in his childhood. I had to grieve the fact that he died when I was only twenty-four and never got to know him as an adult. I reasoned that had he lived longer, I could have, perhaps, helped him in some way or, at least, established some kind of relationship with him.

Recently, I asked my heavenly Father in prayer to help me remember the good things about my father so that I could heal completely and put my hurt in the past. When I would talk about my father and how his lack of building an emotional bond with me had affected my life, Arley would say, "He provided for you. He made a good living as a railroad engineer." That he did. But I guess I must have taken that as a given. Now, I realize what a blessing it was to have a father who cared enough for us to work hard and turn over his paycheck to his family. He didn't have to do that. Even though I had felt abandoned emotionally, he never physically abandoned us or left us to flounder financially.

Once the door was open, I started remembering dancing on his shoes, as many daughters did back in those days. He was over six feet tall, and I'm sure I felt like a feather to him. Dad was a good dancer. He was also smart. He grew up during the

Great Depression and never had a chance to go to college. He had always wanted to be a lawyer. He liked to discuss current events and politics with people when he went downtown Parsons to pay the bills or sit at the soda fountain. I remember people telling me as a child how intelligent he was.

When it would snow, it always prompted Dad to recite the poem "Snowbound" by John Greenleaf Whittier in a very dramatic voice. I have always loved that poem because Dad explained to me what it meant in the difficult places. When I would teach it in American Literature, I would always think of him. Maybe that's where my love of poetry started.

I graduated from college in 1967. He provided me with financial support to go to college at a time when women were supposed to be content with staying home and raising children. Without that degree I wouldn't have been able to have had my twenty-six year teaching career. That has really made a difference in my life. My mother had always said that Dad was proud of me, but I never heard him say it. I couldn't get past all of his anger when I was a child. I guess it didn't sink in that he was showing his love for us by working hard and supporting us financially. In the midst of our pain, it is difficult to understand the pain of the other person.

After writing the book about my mother's Alzheimer's disease, I went back to my hometown of Parsons, Kansas. I was invited by a former high school classmate and friend to speak at a dinner for the women of the Methodist Church there. It was so special because relatives, friends, and neighbors showed up to support me. I talked to everyone and signed books after the talk. Toward the end of my visit, an elderly gentleman came up to me and said that he had worked on the railroad with my father. My parents were around thirty-seven when I was born. They were born in 1909. What were the chances that someone was still alive who had known my father well enough to tell me about him after all these years? The elderly gentleman was ninety-one years old and very clear minded. The conversation went something like this:

"I used to work with your dad on the railroad many years ago. He was a fine man and very smart."
"Did you know him well?"
"Yes, I worked with him quite often."
"Did he ever talk about his family?"
"He was a clean living man. Railroaders have many chances to be unfaithful to their wives. Your father was never like that, as far as I know."
"What about us kids? Did he ever talk about us?"
"Yes, he talked about you three all the time. He was very proud of all of you."

I thanked him, and then called him the day after I got home to tell him why our meeting was so important to me. It was like hearing from my father over forty years after his passing. I went home to Parsons in hopes that I would help someone who was dealing with a friend or loved one with Alzheimer's disease and to tell them how my relationship with Christ had helped me through this trying time. Hopefully, I did. But I was given a gift that evening too. I was on my way to being emotionally and spiritually healed, but God gave me this wonderful gift anyway.

My father had his faults, but I'm not perfect either. We will never be perfect in this life. We will always make mistakes and have to ask God for forgiveness. That is the beauty of Christianity. We can start a new day every day because of the grace and love of our heavenly Father.

Questions to Consider

(1) Why do you think Judith had so much trouble remembering the good things about her father?

(2) What were some of the good things she remembered?

(3) Why did she feel she had to ask God to help her remember?

(4) Why did she consider meeting the man who had worked with her father such a gift?

(5) What did she find out about her father?

(6) How did this change her view of him?

(7) What did she learn about herself?

Chapter 6

Numbing the Pain

"The children in the dysfunctional family may experience high levels of emotional pain. This pain may result from physical or sexual abuse, or it may simply result from the emotional strain of living in an environment that is usually tense and uncertain. In this type of situation, children may adopt compulsive behaviors to keep from feeling the pain. For example, a child growing up in a dysfunctional family discovers that if he stays busy, he does not notice his emotional pain. Carrying this pattern into adulthood, he becomes a work addict. His compulsive work keeps him from feeling inner pain. When he stops working, he feels depressed."[14]

In Robert McGee's book, *The Search for Significance*, he makes the point that in order to heal, we must take steps to look at ourselves in an honest way. He says, "Many of us are hurt emotionally, relationally, spiritually, but because we are unaware of the extent of our wound, we don't take steps toward healing and health."[15] Even after examining ourselves, with or without professional help, we still need to turn to God for spiritual healing. "We need the guidance from the Holy Spirit and usually the honesty, love, and encouragement of at least one other person who is willing to help us."[16] When we do reach an understanding, we will discover that we have tried to meet certain needs in the wrong way. "It isn't that the needs are not real, it is just that we have tried to meet these needs in inappropriate ways."[17]

At some point in our lives, we must all cry out to our heavenly Father. "Search me, O God, and know my heart; test me and know my anxious thoughts. See if there is any offensive way in me, and lead me in the way everlasting." (Psalms 139:23-24) Often this is a painful process, but we must be willing to go through it to find that "peace that passeth all understanding" that we are promised in the Bible. Nothing will fill the hole in our heart, except God's love, grace, and forgiveness.

After many years of soul searching, I realized that I was still that "scared little rabbit" who was trying to cover it all up with outward appearances and constant activity. In high school I tried out for junior varsity cheerleader and could barely eat for a week until I made the squad. I danced in recitals and was an acrobatic twirler in drum corps. In junior college I got honors in scholastic achievement. The last two years of college away from home, I joined a sorority and let my grades slip. Yes, I was the chameleon who could be anything you wanted me to be. "We find it difficult to open up and reveal our inner thoughts and needs because we believe others will reject us if they know what we're really like."[18] It is the feeling that we must meet standards set by others in order to feel good about ourselves.

My first husband Rob and I were living in Iola, Kansas, and I had just finished my first two years of teaching high school English. Now, I wanted to get started on my Master's degree in Secondary Counseling. One of my professors said that if we felt we needed counseling in some area that we should talk to him or one of the other counselors. I made an appointment. Since I was early for my appointment, I decided to go to the ladies room and sit for a while. It was in the autumn of the year, and so I sat on the wide window ledge of that old building with the bathroom on one side. On the other side was the view of all the college activity and the unforgiving ground below. As I looked out that third story window, I thought that hitting the ground wouldn't hurt much more than the pain I was feeling. Something pulled me toward life. I know that my heavenly Father protected me, even though I didn't recognize it at the time.

All this reminds me of a line I wrote in a poem when I was younger: "I am the mechanical ballerina on my mother's music box, dizzy from performing." I walked around with a big hole in my heart that God's love could have filled. He would have accepted me by grace and not by works, but I didn't find that out for many years. Like my earthly father, I was stunted in my ability to give and receive love. If I seemed okay to other people, somehow I felt I could prove that I was okay to myself. It just took more and more achieving to fill that void, but the pain was still there. It becomes an addiction. The more you achieve, the more you need to achieve because there is only momentary satisfaction, and then we are alone once again with ourselves and our pain from childhood. We can look good on the outside and be crumbling on the inside. We build walls between ourselves and others. Walls shut out the pain, but they also shut out the love, especially the openness to the love of God and the healing we can have in our lives by being honest with ourselves, not being stuck in the past, and the willingness and courage to move forward.

Questions to Consider

(1) Why do some people develop compulsive behaviors to numb the pain from childhood?

(2) Name several types of compulsive behaviors.

(3) What does it mean that sometimes we try to meet real needs in an inappropriate way.

(4) Name some examples in which people try to meet emotional needs in the wrong way.

(5) Why is self-discovery such a painful process?

(6) Why it is better to begin our journey to healing as young as possible?

(7) Why is it difficult to open up and reveal our true selves to others?

(8) Should we trust everyone with our innermost thoughts? Why or why not?

(9) How can achieving and approval seeking become an addiction?

(10) Why do we build walls between ourselves and others? What are we afraid of?

Chapter 7

Only God Can Make Us Real

S ome time ago, I stumbled across a book for children called the *Velveteen Rabbit* by Margery Williams. The main character of the book is a little, stuffed rabbit, all shiny and new, who goes through the process of becoming "real," that is, more than just a toy on the shelf. As he struggles with those initial feelings of uneasiness, he engages an old, worn-out, well-used, much-loved stuffed horse in conversation.

"What is REAL?" The Rabbit asked one day, when they were lying side by side near the nursery fender, before Nana came to tidy the room. "Does it mean having things that buzz inside you and a stick-out handle?"

"Real isn't how you are made," said the Skin Horse. "It's something that happens to you. When a child loves you for a long time, not to play with, but REALLY loves you, then you become real."

The Skin Horse goes on to tell him that becoming real takes a very long time, and that by the time you are real, you have become very shabby. He also says, "But these things don't matter at all, because once you are real you can't be ugly, except to people who don't understand."[18]

After reading this story, I quickly realized that I was just the "scared little rabbit" from childhood who became the

Velveteen Rabbit in early adulthood. Now that I'm in my sixties, I feel more like the Skin Horse. I never would have imagined when I was younger that I would be more at peace with myself when my youthful beauty was only a memory. Like the Skin Horse, I am content with having my sharp edges loved off by the important people in my life. Like the Skin Horse said, becoming real takes a long time, but I even know people my age who are unhappy because they haven't found real meaning in their life through a personal relationship with God. Only God can reveal our true selves to us in a way that we know we are forgiven but still very much loved. Only God can make us real.

Questions to Consider

(1) According to the story, *The Velveteen Rabbit,* how do we become real?

(2) What did Judith mean that she was a scared little rabbit in childhood and became the Velveteen Rabbit as a young adult?

(3) Have you ever known anyone who used material things or achievements to hide their true feelings to make others think that everything is OK?

(4) Why would they do this?

(5) Why do people build walls?

(6) How can the love of God and other Christians help us break down these walls?

Part 1
Going Deeper

(1) How would you describe your present relationship or lack of relationship with your father?

(2) What events, actions, attitudes, or words influenced that relationship?

(3) Have you ever talked to your father **through** someone else?

(4) What prevented you from talking to him directly?

(5) What good things do you remember about your father?

(6) How have your father's actions affected who you are today? Explain.

(7) Who gave you approval as a child? Who gives you approval today? How?

(8) Have you ever tried to meet a real need in a destructive or an inappropriate way? What were the results?

(9) Has God ever acted in the role of your heavenly Father and you failed to recognize it? Explain.

Responding to Scripture

How do the following apply to you and your life?

Cast all your anxiety on him because he cares for you. (1 Peter 5:7)

Search me, O God, and know my heart;
*   test me and know my anxious thoughts.*
See if there is any offensive way in me,
*   and lead me in the way everlasting.* (Psalms 139:23-24)

What is impossible with men is possible with God. (Luke 18:27)

And my God will meet all your needs according to his glorious riches in Jesus Christ. (Philippians 4:19)

For I am convinced that neither death nor life, neither angels nor demons, neither the present nor the future, nor any powers, neither height nor depth, nor anything else in all creation, will be able to separate us from the love of God that is in Christ Jesus our Lord. (Romans 8:38)

Part Two
Hiding the Shame

by

Judith David

Chapter 8
Hiding the Shame

People often talk about being brought up in a dysfunctional family but are not always fully aware of exactly what that means. No human being is perfect; therefore, no family is perfect or fully functioning. The degree to which the family is dysfunctional is the degree to which the children are affected. A common dysfunctional family situation is one in which all the attention is focused on one of the family members because of an addiction or mental illness. This is what happened in my family of origin. We were so focused on not upsetting my father that my emotional needs as a child were unmet. My mother did an excellent job of giving us unconditional love and acceptance, but she alone couldn't make up for the lack of a male role model.

A child growing up in a dysfunctional family situation learns to "stuff" their feelings. I didn't want to express anger in the fear that it would make my father even more upset. When I did express any real feelings, my mother would say, "That's not like you." or "Don't get mad." She needed me to be **her** moral support, **her** little counselor. Anger is a normal emotion that children need to process and learn how to control. If the emotions are ignored, the children grow up believing that their feelings aren't important. This usually translates into the feeling that **I** am not important.

In addition, dysfunctional families don't openly talk about their problems, even when everyone knows that a definite problem exists. It's like ignoring the 900 pound gorilla in the room. "Everyone has problems. Conflict is a normal part of family life. In a healthy emotional environment, conflict can be discussed. Solutions can be developed. Hurt feelings can be treated with loving care."[1]

Children like me never learned to solve family problems in a logical manner. Later on as an young adult, I was afraid to speak up if someone hurt my feelings. Then later, I would get angry out of proportion to what the situation warranted because I didn't even ask them to explain what they meant. Since I was taught that it was not okay to express anger, even in an appropriate way, I would keep it all inside. Eventually, the resentment toward that person would build up until I didn't even want to be around them anymore. When this happens again and again, it is a big blow to a young person's self-esteem. Friendships become superficial or short-lived. Intimate relationships are challenging, if not impossible. I think this is the reason I got on the treadmill of being achievement oriented to get approval from those around me because I didn't know how to share my feelings so that a normal, healthy relationship could grow.

I have a very good friend of thirty years named Johanna. She has taught me what true friendship is really like. We have grown in maturity over the years together and have loved each other like sisters, as she has always said, "Warts and all." Without even realizing it, she could look at my expressions and tell that I didn't understand something or was hurt by something, and then she would just merely explain it. When I learned that I could say what I thought without being condemned or abandoned, I started opening up to her and other people. What came so naturally to her took me many years to learn because I hadn't learned to process my feelings as child. We still share a friendship that I will treasure until the day I die. God sends those people into our lives to show us His love.

Children who grew up in dysfunctional families experience a great deal of shame and often can't pinpoint the root of that shame. "Shame is the deep-seated feeling that something is fundamentally wrong with me."[2] Shame is different from guilt. Shame is about what someone else has done to you. Guilt is about what you have done. We have to take responsibility for that and ask forgiveness when we are wrong. Shame is different. "Shame tells you to work your way to acceptability, tells you to apologize for hurting, defies emotional closeness to other people, and promotes an acceptance of inferior relationships. Shame from what you experienced as a child can lead to shame of your own."[3]

As children grow up, this father hunger can produce one of two extremes. Some women try to numb the pain by not feeling anything. Others turn to some form of compulsive behavior and look for some stimulus that will outweigh the internal pain.[4]

Often we try to ease the shame through our behavior by being an approval seeker or perfectionist. "We might also try to numb our pain through compulsive behaviors such as addictions to alcohol, drugs, sex, relationships, or activities like sports or even work. We wear many masks to hide our shame. The Lord desires truth and honesty at the deepest level, and wants us to experience His love in all areas of our lives."[5] Some people call it self-esteem while others call it self-worth, but "the feeling of significance is crucial to man's emotional, spiritual, and social stability and is the driving element within the human spirit."[6]

The multigenerational nature of the impact of family dysfunction is another sad aspect. In the book, *Love is a Choice,* the authors explain the cycle in this way: "The serious dysfunction in a founding family will be absorbed by the children's families, a ripple of misery extending farther and farther down through the years. The dependency or dysfunction may change: an alcoholic father may sire, for instance, a workaholic son who sires a compulsive daughter who spends her way to bankruptcy. But it's always wreaking damage."[7]

Questions to Consider

(1) What are the characteristics of a dysfunctional family? Is there such a thing as a perfect family? Why or why not?

(2) How does living in a dysfunctional family situation affect the emotional growth of a child?

(3) How does growing up in a dysfunctional family affect a child's self-worth?

(4) How important is a feeling of self-worth?

(5) Why do children growing up in a dysfunctional family take on the shame of other family members?

(6) What is father hunger?

(7) How do some young women try to cope with the feelings of father hunger when they reach dating age?

(8) How can family dysfunction be passed down from one generation to the next?

(9) Can the cycle be broken? How?

Chapter 9

Marilyn's Story: Winning the Battle

When I was around thirteen, my mother came upstairs to my room, handed me a book about menstruation, and said, "Don't have sex." I didn't have sex willingly for the first time. In the summer of 1960, my first rape occurred at age fourteen by someone who was supposed to be my friend. In the fall of 1960, the second rape happened when I accepted a ride from an older man while walking home from school. I had violated my parents' moral code, even though it really wasn't my fault. I didn't say anything to my parents either time because, in my mind, I knew they would blame me for it. If my parents had known, I didn't think I would be acceptable to them anymore. So I took the blame and shame and buried the "secret," thus starting my downward spiral. Throughout high school, I tried to find love and acceptance anyway I could. I made myself available for the older guys who wanted sex, which became my way of life. I thought that they wanted me for who I was, and I confused sex with love.

During one year in school, I was invited to two junior proms by two different boys at two different schools. I felt happy because someone thought enough to invite me to a dance, instead of the back seat of a car. The happiness was short-lived because my parents would not have anything to do with helping me get ready for these proms. When I think about those times, I realize that I do not remember anything about leaving the house or the prom itself. Because my parents chose not to be involved in those events, it is the only thing that has stuck with me all these many, many years.

After the rapes I looked at my parents differently, as I was fighting urges I didn't understand and thus became rebellious toward them. I felt alienated from those who gave birth to me. Sometimes I wonder how I would have turned out if those rapes hadn't happened, but they did.

Looking back, I feel that my dad, mostly, was emotionally absent. Positive encouragement was never expressed in our house from either my mom or my dad. Nothing I did was right, according to them. We had talks quite often though it was more two against one, and sometimes they would bring in the preacher. I often stormed to my room in tears. If they had realized what was really going on in my life, I don't think they would have known how to deal with it.

According to the NIV Concordance, Grace is defined as "God's free and unmerited favor for sinful humanity." I always like to think of God as the God of second chances. In my case, He was the God of second, third, and fourth chances. As a matter of fact, as humans we need his grace every day for a continued newness of life and a closer relationship with Him.

When I was thirteen, I "went forward" in church during revival and was baptized because I thought it was what my parents expected me to do. As I reflect back on my life, I wasn't truly baptized into the spirit. I merely got wet. Because of the trauma of the two rapes, the baptism didn't mean a thing to me. I continued to live my life as my desires led me to live it with no thought of the sins I was committing. The more I lived this life, the more discouraged I became. I couldn't find the happiness and contentment I longed for, and my self-hate continued to grow.

When I was old enough, I went to the bars every night "looking for love." I thought that alcohol made me sexy and attractive. Boy was I wrong. All it got me was a "one night stand." I was lucky that I didn't get pregnant until I was twenty-one. I don't remember when I got on the pill. Before I got pregnant, I contracted a sexual disease that was being passed around within the group I was "hanging out" with. When I wasn't married, I continued my partying lifestyle. The more I lived this life, the more discouraged I became and the less I found what I was looking for.

After several challenging marriages, I came to the end of my rope. How could I have chosen the right man to have a healthy relationship with when I had no idea what a healthy relationship was supposed to be like? I was spiraling downward, drowning in self-defeat and felt I had nowhere to go but up. As I write this, I'm in tears for what Jesus did for me and how God has been with me throughout all of this. I'm also in tears for the wasted time I spent away from a right relationship with God. I now know that the voice I always felt inside of me during my old life was that of the Holy Spirit telling me the right thing to do, but I never listened.

I was re-baptized and made a feeble attempt at a Christian life. I still had some of my old ways that I couldn't shake but struggled to live a moral and upright life. As time passed, I finally had enough of making the same mistakes over and over and decided to seek professional guidance from a Christian counselor. I decided that I was the problem and not everyone else, and that it was about time that I break the cycle because I knew that I was passing on the dysfunction to my children. That broke my heart.

I had to start peeling back the layers of defenses and doubt to get rid of the hurt and anger I had been carrying around with me. I first had to process my feelings about the rapes. Then I had to work on why I had made all the self-destructive choices in my past, and why I couldn't make a commitment in my marriages. I met with three different counselors/therapists at various times during my journey of self-discovery. I finally reached the bottom of my downward spiral. I once heard a pastor say that when we are born, we have a sash or ribbon with the words, "I Am Loveable" on it. As we experience pain, shame, hurt, and anger, pieces of the sash are ripped away, and some of us end up with just a thread around us.

My question to myself at the present time concerns what effect my past behavior has had on my children. I've had several marriages that were non-committal on my part that, I know, have had an effect on my children, as well as myself. I went through life not knowing about true love and feeling like I'm lost and the only one on the island. Relationships have been difficult for me and still are to this day.

Even though I have broken the cycle of dysfunction in my life, it still has had an effect on my children. My oldest daughter was eight when her dad and I divorced, the second daughter was five, and the youngest one was a year and a half. During their lifetime, two of them followed in my footsteps and had unhealthy marriage relationships. A third daughter struggles with whether or not she even wants to get married and has decided never to have children. I believe they all struggle with identity and self-worth issues. One is going through her second divorce. My youngest son was greatly affected by the vicious cycle I was caught up in. His dad and I had little respect for one another.

My son was four when his dad and I divorced. Various forms of addiction were present in the household. I remember a moment in time when my son told me he wanted to stand up to his dad, but he needed me to be there for him. He was just too scared to do this alone. I still remember the day. His dad just laughed at us and tried to turn the blame on my son. After years of struggle with his own addiction, my son ended up committing suicide at the age of nineteen from a drug overdose.

There was a ten year period of time I chose to stay single and not make the destructive choices I had made earlier in my life. I had learned not to trust myself where relationships were concerned and was really happy being single. Then I met someone who actually had an interest in me and wanted to get to know me for who I was. He treated me with respect. He treated me like a lady. I learned to love him for the giving and accepting person that he was. This was a new experience for me. We gave ourselves time to get to know each other and then were married. After a short marriage, he died, and I am still grieving his loss. I know that he loved me and I loved him, like no other. I learned that I can love and be loved when I let God lead. I sometimes wonder why I had to lose the love of my life after I finally got my life straightened out. After this past year without him, I know that I am sufficient all by myself. But I'm not really by myself, and God's love in me is sufficient.

I did not have a moment in time that God changed me overnight. He placed me on a journey of several years. Looking back, I realize that God was by my side the whole time. He put incredible people in my life at the precise time who would love me in spite of where I had been and what I had done. I can now throw myself at His feet and give Him my anger, hurts, disappointments, and all the emotional baggage I have been carrying around my whole life. He extends His love and grace to me in spite of how long it took me to get to the foot of the cross. He knew I was struggling to get to Him. Even though I turned away from Him many times, He never left me. He was with me during the time I grieved the death of my youngest son. He was also with me when I grieved the death of my husband. During this time, He sent my Christian brothers and sisters from church to be His hands, feet, and mouth to carry me though those desperate times.

HIS GRACE IS SUFFICIENT EVEN FOR ME. I know that He will not give me any more than I can handle, and that He will provide a way through any struggle. Like all people, I will continue to learn and grow until the day I die. My journey now is of a different kind. I know that I am a child of His and that I am forgiven. I do not have to carry the guilt of my sins anymore because they are nailed to the cross. I am free to love myself and others because I know He loves and accepts me.

Over those sick years, I couldn't even look at myself in the mirror because of the guilt, shame, and feelings of worthlessness. I now love myself as God loves me, and I choose to walk that path daily. Recently, a man asked me to go with him for the weekend, which would involve an overnight stay. I just calmly said, "No, I can't. I'm a Christian." Now I can set my boundaries and know that it's okay. Now I see clearly and make choices according to God's plan.

Questions to Consider

(1) How did Marilyn's two rapes at a young age affect her relationship with her parents?

(2) How did it affect her self-worth?

(3) How did she try to find love and acceptance?

(4) Describe Marilyn's relationship with her father.

(5) How did Marilyn's relationship with her father affect her relationship with others, especially men?

(6) How did Marilyn numb her emotional pain?

(7) How did her lifestyle affect her feelings of self-worth?

(8) Why do you think her marriages and family relationships were challenging?

(9) Why didn't she listen to that "voice inside her"?

(10) What do you think that "voice inside her" was?

(11) What do you think caused her downward spiral?

(12) Was there anything she could have done to keep her from "hitting rock bottom"?

(13) According to the NIV Concordance, grace is defined as "God's free and unmerited favor for sinful humanity." What is grace? How did God's grace help her turn away from her sinful life?

(14) Why does Marilyn worry about the effect her former lifestyle might have had on her own children?

(15) Does she have reason to worry?

(16) Why do you think she continues to struggle with relationships? With God's help, do you think her relationships will continue to improve?

(17) What effect has Marilyn's family dysfunction had on her adult children?

(18) Can this generational cycle be broken? How?

(19) How did her healthy relationship with her late husband change the view she had of herself?

(20) How have Marilyn's present day relationships helped her through the grief process after her husband's death?

Chapter 10

Chastity, Loss of Virginity, and Forgiving Yourself

W omen who have never had a healthy relationship with a father often have problems with intimate relationships. Sometimes they look for the love they never received from their father in other men. Often their expectations are unrealistic. They either expect too much or too little. They may also equate sex with love.

"Father Hunger is a very strong drive. Women caught up in this dynamic are willing to sacrifice everything to secure their (emotional) heart's desire."[8] For some women father hunger can be stronger than the strongest narcotic. Because little girls learn to be feminine in contrast to the way their fathers behave in a masculine way, emotions are warped when this normal interaction fails to occur.[9]

A few years before I retired from teaching, the high school had a lady speaker who discussed the reasons for abstinence. She had been a model and had some connection with the movie industry. She was young, and I suppose the speaker's bureau felt like she could reach teenagers with her message. The opposite was true.

I stayed in my classroom to grade papers, and when the students started filing back to class, I asked them about the assembly. They said that they didn't get any good reasons for abstinence because all she did was talk about her accomplishments.

I was an older teacher, and I think that the class was surprised that I would even broach the subject. I think I even surprised myself. I gave them a practical answer. I told them that boys were at their sexual peak around eighteen, and that sex dominated their thoughts a great deal of their waking hours. Girls, on the other hand, were more prone to think about dating as a way of choosing her future husband. After sex a girl might envision how the closeness would strengthen their bond. The boy might just be thinking that he sure felt better and wanted more of the same.

At that comment the girls stared daggers at the boys while the boys looked sheepish and slouched down into their desks. I went on to explain that this did not mean that boys didn't have feeling like girls, but that they just viewed sex differently. I told them that having sex and then later on breaking up with a boy may leave emotional scars that might take years to remove. Several members of the class agreed that they learned more from my explanation than they had during the assembly.

Dr. Louann Brizendine in her book named *The Female Brain* explains what she calls The Great Sexual Divide. "Men, quite literally, have sex on their minds more than women do. Males have double the brain space and processing power devoted to sex as females. Just as women have an eight-lane superhighway for processing emotion while men have a small country road, men have O'Hare Airport as a hub for processing thoughts about sex whereas women have the airfield nearby that lands small private planes. That probably explains why 85 percent of twenty- to thirty-year-old males think about sex many times each day and women think about it once a day—up to three or four times on their most fertile days. This makes for interesting interactions between the sexes. Guys often have to talk women into having sex. It's not usually the first thing on women's minds."[10]

Everyone makes mistakes, especially when they're young. In the movie *The Passion of the Christ*, I saw the sinful woman who was caught in the act of adultery and brought in by the Pharisees to stand before a group gathered in the temple court. According to law, the punishment was death by stoning. Everyone knows what happened after that. Jesus says to the crowd, "If anyone of you is without sin, let him be the first to throw a stone at her." After all are gone, Jesus asks her, "Woman, where are they? Has no one condemned you?" She replies, "No one, sir." Jesus then declares, "Then neither do I condemn you. Go now and leave your life of sin." (John 8:1-11)

Watching the movie, I saw the condemned woman desperately crawling toward Christ to touch His feet or perhaps the hem of His garment. I saw the look on her face and felt what she must have felt, the transforming power of Christ's grace and forgiveness. The sinful woman was from the lowest rung of society, and people had considered her unclean her entire life. Have you ever had someone stand up for you when everyone else was against you? I have. I remember how I felt toward the person who believed in me. I will never forget them. Can you imagine how the sinful woman felt when no one had held her in high esteem her entire life, and then He who was pure, holy, and without sin saw her as clean and forgave her? She had probably not experienced unconditional love from a man who wanted nothing but to save her soul.

We have all done things in our past, especially in our youth, that we are not proud of. They may not be really horrible, in some cases, but we wouldn't want these transgressions posted on the internet. I have always been my own worst critic, at times paralyzed by guilt and shame. It has always been easier for me to forgive other people than it has been to forgive myself. This pattern of self-condemnation and shame has caused me to walk around with a heavy burden in my heart. In our head we may know that we are forgiven, but in our hearts we are not sure that we deserve that forgiveness. After viewing this scene, I finally came to the conclusion that if God extends his grace and forgiveness to us, all we have to do is to take it. It's like when my father couldn't believe that we kids really loved him. Our love was there, but he couldn't accept it. Why do we keep beating ourselves up over and over again? Why can't we forgive ourselves? If God says in the Bible that He will forgive us for each and every sin we have committed, then we know for sure that He will do it.

A stone sits on the table in the foyer of our church just before entering the main sanctuary. On it are written the words from this story of the sinful woman, "He who is without sin should cast the first stone." No one has picked it up; it still remains there today.

Questions to Consider

(1) Why do some women equate sex with love?

(2) Why is father hunger such a strong drive?

(3) Why is the father/daughter relationship so important?

(4) How do men and women view sex differently?

(5) How do the male and female brains process sex differently? Why?

(6) Why was the sinful woman so affected by Jesus' attitude toward her?

(7) How does Jesus demonstrate grace towards the sinful woman in the story?

(8) Even though Jesus forgave her, does He still expect her to change her lifestyle?

(9) Why is it hard for some people to accept love, grace, and forgiveness from others?

(10) Why is it hard for some people to accept love, grace, and forgiveness from our heavenly Father?

Chapter 11

Karen's Story: The Way Home

I am the oldest child in a family of three children. I was born in a small town in Kansas and grew up the poor child of a dairy farmer. There wasn't much money to go around, and since my mother had to work in the field and the dairy barn, I had a lot of responsibility with the household duties and taking care of the younger children. My father was in WWII and never had much use for Christianity. My mother, however, was brought up in a Christian home, and she was a strong Christian woman who always made sure that I attended church. I accepted the Lord as my Savior and was baptized at the age of nine.

We moved around a lot, and I only went the entire school year in one school during the first grade and the twelfth grade. The rest of the time I went to as many as five schools in one school year. I never really knew why we moved so much. Mom always said that Dad had itchy feet.

Life seemed pretty normal until I was about thirteen years old, and suddenly my father started to sexually molest me. I don't really have any idea what set it all in motion. Who knows why people do the terrible things that they do. The sexual molestation continued until I was approximately eighteen years of age. I don't want to go into a lot of detail because that's not why I'm writing this. I am writing this with the hope that someone out there will read this and profit from my experiences.

After talking to several women, I have become aware that in my small circle of friends, there are so many women who have been sexually molested, and we are still hiding in the closet for fear of condemnation. We are afraid of no longer being accepted. We are afraid of losing other women's trust. We are told that it's our fault. If we had just done something different, it wouldn't have happened. Children are not responsible for the actions of the adults around them. It is not your fault and don't let anyone convince you otherwise. After all of these years, I have finally come to realize that I am not a victim, rather I am Victorious. I will not allow myself to get trapped in the past.

It is really amazing the things with which children can learn to deal. In that period of time, this was a skeleton in the family closet, and these things weren't talked about. I was warned to keep quiet or suffer the consequences. I know that I told a couple of teachers at school, but I guess no one took me seriously. I tried to commit suicide a couple of times with pills. I wasn't successful at that. God had other plans for me. I ran away from home a couple of times. That is kind of humorous since we lived in rural areas and how far could you get before they found you? That was in the 50's. There weren't any child protection laws in force like there are in current times. You couldn't call up DHS and turn your father in or at least I didn't know about it if there was such a thing. In my mind, I was trapped. I never got to be a kid. I had to grow up very fast. There was always the pressure to keep the secret.

One time when we were moving, we were taking more than one vehicle, and I didn't want to ride with my dad. Dad must have been trying to convince me to ride with him. At any rate, my mom became suspicious and wanted to know why I didn't want to ride with my dad. I tried to put her off, but she kept asking more questions. I finally broke down and told her what was going on. Well, that lead to a big confrontation. The three of us sat down in the living room, and it seemed like it just happened yesterday. When my dad was confronted, he lied about it and said that it wasn't true, and it must just have been a misunderstanding. I guess my mother believed him because we never talked about it after that. Of course, for it to come out in the open would be a great embarrassment for a Southern Baptist wife and mother. So I guess she needed to protect her image more than she needed to protect me. She kept telling me how much she loved me, and as a child I thought she did love me. I didn't want to hurt her by bringing it up every time he touched me. So, I never said anything else about it since it was obvious that she wasn't going to do anything about it.

I learned to be very aware of my surroundings. I tried to always be ahead of any situation that would leave me alone with him. I became very active in extracurricular activities that kept me away from home. I dated a lot and tried to stay away from home as much as possible. I acted out and became promiscuous. At the time I didn't understand what the underlying reason was for my actions. I caused my mother a lot of heartache since I wasn't the good little girl that she expected me to be, and now I know that we probably did a lot of moving around so that there weren't any long term relationships that would reveal what was happening in my home life.

It's very difficult to talk about where my mother was in all of this. I will never understand why she chose to ignore what was happening. I was talking to her one day on the phone after I had been married several years, and she made the statement that God had forgiven me. Why couldn't I forgive myself? That comment haunted me for a long time. I wasn't the one who needed forgiveness. But I have finally realized that it's not my job to psychoanalyze her or her motives. We can't change anything except ourselves and our actions. Therefore, it's about you and your relationship with the one and only one that you can depend on. The One who loves you no matter what—GOD!

It has taken me many years and a lot of soul searching to get to the point where I am today. It is sad to think that I have wasted so many years being angry, bitter, resentful, not trusting people and building a wall around my heart to try to prevent any more hurt. And all that time, I wasn't even aware. I thought I was right, and everyone else was wrong. I never saw these things in myself for years. I had to tear down the wall before I could see myself for what I really was.

Well, enough of the whining. NO more gloom and doom. I wanted to share some things with you that I have learned from this experience and move into the sunshine. The greatest thing that my mother did for me was taking me to church. I learned about Jesus at an early age and accepted Him as my Savior. That doesn't mean that I always turned to Him when I should have, but I believe that He was still looking out for me and protecting me from harm. I believe that God said, "You are my child. You may turn away from me, but I will never turn away from you. I will be here waiting when you call on my name." He is Mighty and Faithful through it all. It is hard to understand just how much God loves us when He is compared to our earthy fathers. His love and faithfulness has no bounds. He will never forsake you.

The people who know me best say, "You are an amazing woman." However, I say my God is amazing. He has given me the opportunity to raise two young boys into great men, free from the sickness and twistedness of their forefather and to be married to an amazing man who has seen me through all the emotional and spiritual pain and suffering in this life. Praise God for providing us with the promise of redemption and deliverance from the sin and evil of this world. I am a child of the one and only living God, the King of Kings.

The Wayward Child
by
Judith David

That day the warm shower of Your love
came pouring down to save me from my sins.
I fell to my knees broken and in silence
and vowed to stay
in the light of the Living Word
and in the warmth of Your presence,
grasping Your loving hand.

The Great Deceiver laughed
because he knew my weaknesses
and dangled temporal pleasures of the world
before my childish eyes.

Like the wayward child I was,
I broke loose my grasp
to taste the pleasures of the earth.

The ice cream was rich and smooth.
The candy lingered sweet upon my tongue.
My eyes lusted after brightly colored balloons
that bounced softly in the autumn breeze.

But much too soon—
The ice cream melted into nothingness.
The sweetness of the candy left me wanting more.
The balloons floated recklessly
as autumn tugged at winter.

And much too soon—
A cold gust of wind
came out of the cold gray clouds
and jerked them from my grasp.
Some broke against
rough asphalt
sharp corners
and leafless tree branches.

The rest grew smaller and smaller
and faded into the distance.
As the last one disappeared from view,
I raised my fist in the anger of a childish tantrum,
then beat my hands against the hard wall
of disappointment and despair.

I fell to my knees broken and in silence.
In the cold darkness of my mind,
I saw you, my Savior,
with outstretched arms on the cross
and begged Your forgiveness.

No longer blinded
by the temptations of the world,
I lifted my tear stained face.
I saw Your flowing robes and outstretched arms
and knew You were always there.
I rushed back to you as suddenly as I had left,
and You welcomed me home again.

My precious Lord,
Help me strengthen my faith so that I may always
walk in the light of the Living Word
and in the warm presence of Your everlasting love.

A Fresh Start

In Rick Warren's best-selling book, *The Purpose Driven Life,* he says, "We are products of our past, but we don't have to be prisoners of it. God's purpose is not limited by your past. He turned a murderer named Moses into a leader and a coward named Gideon into a courageous hero, and he can do amazing things with the rest of your life, too. God specializes in giving people a fresh start."[11]

Questions to Consider

(1) Why are women afraid to talk about being raped or molested as a child?

(2) How common do you think it is?

(3) Why do you think that Karen's mother chose to believe her husband rather than Karen?

(4) How did this make Karen feel about herself?

(5) How did this experience affect her feelings of self-worth?

(6) How did this experience affect her relationships later in life?

(7) How did God's love help change her attitude and her heart?

Part 2
Going Deeper

(1) Did you grow up in a dysfunctional family situation?

(2) How has it affected your feelings of self-worth?

(3) How has it affected your relationships?

(4) Have you ever had a secret you were afraid to tell anyone? Why or why not?

(5) Have you ever had someone you love not believe you?

(6) How did it make you feel?

(7) Have you ever had someone stand up for you when no one else was on your side? How did it make you feel?

(8) Have you ever wanted a fresh start?

(9) What is stopping you from getting a fresh start in life?

(10) How can a relationship with your heavenly Father help give you a fresh start?

Responding to Scripture

How do the following scriptures apply to you and your life? Explain.

Therefore, if anyone is in Christ, he is a new creation, the old has gone, the new has come. (2 Corinthians 5:17)

Do not let your hearts be troubled. Trust in God; trust also in me. (John 14:1)

Trust in the Lord with all your heart and lean not on your own understanding; in all your ways acknowledge him, and he will make your paths straight.
(Proverbs 3:5-6)

Never will I leave you:
never will I forsake you. (Hebrews 13:15)

But God demonstrates his own love for us in this: While we were still sinners, Christ died for us. (Romans 5:8)

Part Three
Coming Full Circle

by

Linda M. Smith

Chapter 12
Becoming an Enabler

I was the oldest of eight children. There were five of us, and we were all in school. I was fourteen. Then my mother had Amy, and within eighteen months she was pregnant and had twins. Everyone in the community thought that Amy was mine because I took care of her all the time.

My dad drank a lot. He was also a severe juvenile diabetic. It took me until the age of thirty to realize that he was an alcoholic. One of my great escapes was on Saturday when he was running errands, and Mom would send me with him. I thought it was to give me a break from all the babysitting and housework I had to help with at home, but later I realized that she hoped that this would deter him from drinking. Instead, I would sit on the bar stool next to him and get to know all his friends. We would have lunch almost every Saturday in the local bar.

At age forty-six, I took a Christian counseling class. The class was discussing enablers because we had just watched a video about enablers. An enabler is someone who helps the alcoholic or addicted loved one to avoid the consequences of their actions or destructive choices. During the break, I just sat there as the Holy Spirit began to speak to me and said that I had been trained to be the perfect enabler all my life. With helping to take care of the three babies at home and being sent out to watch Dad when his drinking increased, I knew that I had to keep peace at any cost. Even though I was sent as a spy,

I would never tell on my Dad. Then in the afternoon, Mom would go and do her errands. After we had lunch and the babies were put down for naps, I was always there to help.

Usually around once a month, Dad would not have lunch or drink too much that morning, or whatever the situation, and he would go into a diabetic reaction. And at thirteen, fourteen, or fifteen years old, I had to call the ambulance, protect the younger kids, give him orange juice or sugar, and sometimes fight him to drink it. It was really chaotic. It is ironic that I never thought of my dad as an alcoholic. I thought it was his diabetes until I was old enough to realize that one triggered the other. That's how I became an enabler as a child.

When I got married later on, I was also an enabler for twenty-five years. It was easier not to deal with the issues or to confront the problems going on—to keep things status quo. I wanted to try to make things appear the way they should; in other words, we projected the image of a wonderful church going family to those outside our home. Pressure would build up, and we would reach a breaking point. When we couldn't take it anymore, we would yell and scream. I didn't deal with any issues because my family never dealt with issues when I was growing up. That was the style of communication or lack of communication I had experienced with my parents. After the fight, nobody ever apologized. It was over. That was it. Nothing positive happened, and nothing changed. So that was the cycle I was caught up in all my life. I was raised "daddy's girl." The oldest granddaughter. Dad and I ran around, and we did these things together, but yet there was no deep communication.

When I was in high school, I would work as a waitress after school. I would come home at 10 or 10:30, be exhausted, and get my pajamas on. My dad and I would watch television together. After the news was over, *Perry Mason* (a detective show during the 1960's) would come on, and we would watch it with a box of Cheese-Its. We didn't talk. Everyone was asleep, and I was wound up from work. Even though there was very little communication, to me it was one of my fondest memories. As an adult looking back, I now realize how shallow it was. However, Cheese-Its is still one of my favorite foods.

James Dobson, a well known Christian writer and speaker, talks about adolescent relationships. Going to the movies is one of the worst dates because there is no communication. Watching *Perry Mason* was the same way because we were together, but that was all.

Questions to Consider

(1) What is an enabler?

(2) How did Linda become an enabler in her childhood?

(3) How did Linda continue this pattern into her marriage?

(4) What was the communication pattern between Linda and her father in her childhood?

(5) Do you think she also continued this pattern into her marriage? Why or why not?

Chapter 13

Marrying Someone Like My Father

L ater on, this lack of communication became apparent in my marriage. The Holy Spirit told me that I was the perfect enabler and that this was **my** sin. I can't deal with someone else's addictions or sin, but for me to allow someone else to sin is a sin itself. We need to confront people to deal with these things, especially in our own home in order to develop intimate relationships. That was a hard pill for me to swallow. I knew that if I dealt with it with maturity, a Christian maturity, that I would have to confront him, drawing a line in the sand, and say, "No more!" As a Christian, we must declare, "As for me and my house, we will serve God." I knew that the circumstances the way they were, we were not serving God or serving our relationship. It's not pointing your finger at the other person saying, "These are your sins that cannot be dealt with. It's saying, "This is what I have to do." I knew if I ever took that stand and drew the line in the sand that my whole marriage could come to an end. It took almost two to two and a half years for me to actually do that. I was becoming more miserable as time went on because I knew what God wanted me to do. His sin or demon was addiction; mine was allowing it in my house.

It's amazing because psychologists will tell you that you will marry someone similar to your father. But I thought to myself, "He doesn't drink." However, other addictions have just as much of an impact. Do you know how long it takes us to recognize that it's the same demon? It's the same one but just in a different dress. "We all possess a primal need to re-create the familiar, the original family situation, *even if the familiar, the situation, is destructive and painful.*" It is the magical, highly unrealistic thinking that we can go back now that we are older and correct what was done to us in the past.[1] It is a subconscious desire that plays out over and over again until we go through that long process of self-examination. It is only then that healing will begin, and we can go on to form more healthy relationships.

Over the years, I have worked in several church youth groups and pregnancy centers counseling young girls about unhealthy relationships, pregnancy issues, and childbirth preparation. I am now the director of the Abundant Blessings Center in Grove, Oklahoma. I talk to many girls here at the pregnancy center who come out of abusive relationships. These girls have been beaten down by one bad relationship after another. Some girls and even adult women think that they always have to have a man in their lives. Good counselors, and especially Christian counselors, will tell you that if you come out of a relationship that was not healthy, it will take you around two years to find out who you are so that you won't walk back into that same trap. In the healing process, you might find out that you did marry someone like your father or someone like your ex-husband all over again. It just took on a different form, but it was still the same. I don't think you realize how much those kinds of relationships can tear your self-esteem down. My self-esteem suffered greatly after my divorce, even though I was a strong person who went on to get a college education.

John Stafford, a well-known Christian counselor, has a huge ministry that trains other Christian counselors. They do counseling, and the reason is to bring things up to take them to the cross. They talk about how some of our attributes, deficiencies, and weaknesses can attract or repel other people. Our father might have fulfilled some of our needs in an unhealthy way. If we're not far enough away from the relationship to have those holes in our psyche or personality healed, then we're looking to fill them again. It's amazing how we attract those things, even things we don't want to. We have to allow ourselves enough time to process our feelings, hopefully with a trusted adult, minister, or trained counselor in order to allow Jesus Christ to break the cycle. If we don't allow these wounds to heal from the inside out, we will most likely rush right into another destructive relationship.

Questions to Consider

(1) How did Linda's lack of communication with her father affect her later on?

(2) How did she "draw a line in the sand"?

(3) Why did she feel that she had to do this?

(4) What is "peace at any cost"? Explain.

(5) What does "peace at any cost" cost us? Explain.

(6) Does it sometimes take courage to speak up and share your feelings?

(7) Why do women often marry someone like their father?

(8) Are they always aware that they are doing this?

(9) Can someone seem very different from your father on the surface but be just like him in how he relates to you?

(10) Why would someone who has been abused or neglected as a child marry a man who was abusive, neglectful, or emotionally absent?

(11) Can a father be a good person and still be emotionally absent?

(12) Why do you think some fathers have a great deal of trouble relating to their maturing daughters?

(13) Why is it important to give yourself time to heal after being in a relationship with an abusive, neglectful, or emotionally absent man?

(14) How can counseling, Christian relationships, and a closer walk with God help break this destructive cycle?

Chapter 14

Taking It to the Cross

At nineteen I experienced my first sexual relationship and ended up pregnant within the first eight to ten weeks. Before I even found out I was pregnant, I started seeing great weaknesses in this older man and knew that this relationship was not going to work. I knew I needed out of it and finally left the relationship. What was utterly amazing is how the Holy Spirit leads us and guides us. I didn't know that I was pregnant. He was my boss, and so I lost the relationship and my job at the same time. It was my first sexual relationship, and he was an older man, and early on I thought that he would protect and take care of me and be what I needed. It was probably what I was hoping my father would be. After I left the relationship, all I wanted to do was mope around the house for a couple of weeks. I didn't do much, except cry. I was frustrated with myself and the whole situation. I now know that the Holy Spirit was dealing with me. I didn't know it then. A couple of weeks later, having been raised a good Catholic girl, I went to confession on Good Friday before Easter. I was sick and nauseous, but I thought it was the guilt of being in the relationship and also losing my job. I blamed it all on that.

It took me years to realize that the Holy Spirit was dealing with me so much that I repented of the relationship. As I went to confession, I realized I wasn't just telling someone what I had done. It was a real repentance. I went up to the altar, knelt there, and began to cry out to God for forgiveness. When I became conscious of my surroundings once again, I was kneeling at the foot of the cross that was lying there across the altar for Lent. When I got home, I knew that something drastically different had happened. The weight of the world was off my shoulders. I felt good; I physically felt good. There was a peace on the inside of me.

After that, I knew that I had to go out and find my good friends and tell them that I'm okay and about this life-changing experience. So, I went to the local bar where my friends hung out. I just sat there. I didn't know what had happened to me until years later. I just knew that I felt good. I ordered a drink and couldn't even drink it. I just sat there talking to my friends. My friends asked me if I was high, and I said that I was high on something, but I didn't know what it was. At that point, Jesus had definitely come into my life and things were changed. I knew that things were changed. People knew that things were changed in me, but nobody could explain at that time what it was.

Then about a week or two later, I realized that I was pregnant. I don't know how I would have gotten through it without that life-changing experience. The father image is so important. I made an appointment with our family doctor, who had known me for several years. I was nineteen and made the appointment without telling my parents. When the doctor determined that I was pregnant, he came in himself, instead of sending the nurse. As the tears rolled down my face, it was utterly amazing. He reached over, grabbed my hand, looked at me and said, "The good girls always get caught." These are words I remembered all my life. Now, I realize how important it is what we say to people in a crisis. He was affirming. He said, "If you were out doing this all the time, you'd be on the pill or doing some kind of birth control." Of course, I wish that this was true now, but forty years ago, things were different. But he affirmed me when he gave me the bad news. And that was powerful.

I babysat for a wonderful "born again" couple, and he was a psychiatrist. Somehow, he found out that I was pregnant. When I was about five or six months pregnant, he knocked on the door and asked to speak to me. We sat in the backyard and talked, and he wanted to let me know that he and his wife had been praying for me. They also wanted to know if there was anything they could do for me. They simply asked how I was doing. Father God will send those people into our lives, and it's unfortunate that it takes great hindsight for us to recognize that He was there to give us what we needed all along. That was really awesome.

These two men were a great contrast to my father's silent anger. I went home and didn't say anything for a couple of weeks. Then my mother figured it out and asked me if I was pregnant. My father did not speak to me for six months. We always had very little communication, but now it was even less. He reduced his comments to things like, "Could you pass the bread?" or "Would you pick up the boys?" We didn't talk about what was going on with me. It was really hard. That's how we had always handled problems at our house.

The Holy Spirit kept speaking to me throughout the pregnancy. Thirty years ago, 95% of the girls who got pregnant without being married gave the baby up for adoption, married the father, or got an abortion. Initially, my father put some pressure on me to get married. When I refused, he just shut down. He wouldn't talk to me. In my heart the Holy Spirit let me know that getting pregnant was a onetime sin that could be forgiven. But marriage was a covenant, a lifetime commitment. I didn't understand covenant at the time, but I knew it was a lifetime commitment that I couldn't honor with this man. So, I was very strong, and I now know that the strength came from God. I also had a knowing in my heart that when the baby was born that the reaction of people would be different. As director of the Abundant Blessings Center, this is something that I share with girls all the time. What you see now isn't necessarily what will happen when the baby is born. Sometimes positive reactions turn to negative. For example, the boyfriend you thought would be with you forever is suddenly gone because he can't deal with the baby. Sometimes negative reactions like parents and grandparents turn to positive because you can't deny the precious gift God has given. There's something so unique about new life that is compelling to us as human beings.

Questions to Consider

(1) Why do you think that Linda was attracted to an older man?

(2) Do you think that this attraction had anything to do with father hunger in her childhood? Why or why not?

(3) How does Linda's asking the Lord for forgiveness make her feel changed?

(4) Why do you think other people noticed that she had changed?

(5) How did this change in her help her to cope with her unexpected pregnancy?

(6) How did Linda's father react to her pregnancy?

(7) How did his reaction make her feel?

(8) How did the psychiatrist and his wife react to her pregnancy?

(9) How did this make her feel?

(10) How did the presence of the Holy Spirit give her comfort?

(11) How do we experience the presence of the Holy Spirit?

(12) Is it available to everyone? How?

Chapter 15

Giving Back

It took a few years, but I finally got myself back together trying to do a good job at work. After a while, my mother put pressure on me to start dating. I think she was afraid that she would have to raise me and my son forever if she didn't get me married. I could see and hear it in her attitude that she was anxious for me to get married and get out of the house. I don't know whether it was because my siblings would soon be teenagers, or she genuinely wanted me to get started on my own life. But I started dating and ended up in another sexual relationship. One of the things my dad did say after he started talking to me was that if it ever happened again, I would be out on my rear. In 1973, I found myself pregnant again.

When I went to a local doctor, he said, "Well, you don't have to be pregnant." No explanations. No nothing. And, of course, in January of 1973 with the passage of Roe v Wade, abortion had become very common. I don't even think the doctors understood all the ramifications of that law. I don't think anybody did. There was no disclosure. No information. Apparently, one would just check into the hospital, and when they left, they wouldn't be pregnant anymore. It seemed simple and easy. Nobody said that it would be part of my life forever.

Around the fall of 1973, I had an abortion. I just knew that I had to take care of the child I already had. It's really strange because I just tucked it away in the back of my mind. It was something that wasn't dealt with for a while. I became numb. I'm convinced that my mother knew. I told her that I was going in for a D & C. She had to know what was happening, but she never said a word. We have never talked about it since. Those things shaped my life in ways I didn't even understand at the time.

A year later I was married and got pregnant on my honeymoon. I never did have time to adjust to being married because I was pregnant and caring for a five year old. It all just hit bing, bang, boom. My husband and I were still in the Catholic church but were very much a part of the charismatic renewal in Phoenix. The local priest worked with one of the pregnancy centers. I met some people there, and that's when I started to feel called to do this as my life's work. I had gone through the birth of my first child alone. They wouldn't allow anyone to be in the birthing room when I had my son, not even my mom who had given birth to eight children. Then, of course, I went through the abortion totally alone. That was my motivation. I didn't want anybody to have to go through what I went through alone.

Five years after my first pregnancy, I started working for the first time in a pregnancy center doing outreach and some peer counseling. It was really interesting. Many of the workers there were Catholic, and these ladies read the Bible extensively. They read the Word. That's when I first started reading it. One of them shared a scripture with me and 2 Corinthians 1:37 has become one of my anthems. It says that we should praise God because He comforts us in all our troubles so that we can comfort others because of the comfort we have received from Him. That's why God will use the things in our past for us to minister to other people in the future. Having been there ourselves, we find the comfort of God and the grace of God in our lives, which leads us to help others. It wasn't a planned journey. It wasn't a conscious journey. It was just a feeling: "Yeah, I can do that!"

That was over thirty years ago, and I'm still helping unwed mothers. We don't call them unwed mothers anymore. We call them single moms. It's not just teenagers who are struggling. The face has changed a lot. I see women way up in their thirties coming in with unplanned pregnancies from illicit relationships that are based on bad history. Some have two or three children from two or three different fathers. They have had one bad relationship after another. It's scary what has happened in our society and how not having a constant father figure has really changed. Some young girls bounce from relationship to relationship, and we try to get them to realize that they need to get healthy so that they can identify a healthy relationship. It doesn't happen all the time, but there are small successes. Some go back to school or get their own place. We try to teach them that with the grace of God He can lead them and guide them. Then they can hopefully get into a good and strong healthy relationship along the way.

My experience was so different than what's out there right now. My heart just breaks for these young girls. We have girls ten, eleven, and twelve who feel pressure to engage in sexual activity to be part of a group. The pressure is so overwhelming. At that age, it is so difficult to get them to think about any long term effects because long term to them may be only six months into the future. It's such a different society. The pressure is so unreal. No matter what decision you make, whether it is abortion or placing the child for adoption, it stays with you forever. That is really the main common ground we have. That's what I can share with them.

We're just blown away here at the center when we hear about these really young girls and their attitudes toward sex. I don't know if it's thanks to our wonderful former President

Clinton or not, but they are really convinced that having oral sex is not sex. But the things they are doing are really opening themselves to disease, which can also have long term effects. Sexual activity among our teenagers can be pervasive. We may be only seeing the tip of the iceberg in pregnancy. Schools that are handing out condoms don't see the whole picture of how much is out there. They don't know what happens before a student has a full sexual relationship and how it is damaging their lives.

Questions to Consider

(1) What was Linda's father's reaction to her becoming pregnant again?

(2) How did her father's reaction affect her choices when she experienced another unplanned pregnancy?

(3) What was her doctor's solution?

(4) Why did Linda's emotions become numb after the abortion?

(5) What did she mean by the following statement?

"Those things shaped my life in ways I didn't even understand at the time."

(6) How have things changed for single moms in the past thirty years? (If you don't know, ask your grandmother or some other women in her age group.)

(7) Why do some young women feel they have to be sexually active to be part of some group?

(8) Why does the decision to have an abortion, keep the child, or place the child for adoption stay with you forever?

Chapter 16

The Impact of Godly Men

As director of Abundant Blessings Center, one of my first speaking engagements here in Grove was to a men's church group. Anna Shaw, the director of the Christian H.E.L.P. Center, wasn't available, and so she asked if they would consider having me speak. Since they were a men's group, they didn't see how learning about a pregnancy center in town was relevant. She explained that there are lots of things that they could do to help the pregnancy center. Finally, a week and a half later, they did call me. Maybe they couldn't find anyone else right before Christmas. I don't know. In the meantime, I had been praying, "Lord, what will I tell these men?" Yes, I could tell them that I needed shelves, and I needed people who can haul cribs and furniture to young moms. Of course, it would be nice to have people with trucks to help us. But I knew that these were influential men in our community who could make a difference. I prayed, "God, what would you have me say and do?"

Instantly, there was a replay of three men that made a difference when I found out I was pregnant as a teenager—the doctor, my dad, and the psychiatrist. My father's negative reaction made me feel even worse than I already did. I knew I had to share with them how two other important men in my life made a positive difference in the past and how they too can make a difference in a young person's life today.

The doctor didn't deny that I was pregnant, he didn't deny that I had sex, but he reaffirmed me as a person. That gave me some strength, some courage in the days ahead. The words of the psychiatrist friend who came to my house so many years ago to ask if there was anything he could do, also came to mind. How my own father, not speaking to me and shutting down, affected me. How his statement that if I ever got pregnant again, I would be out on my rear, affected me and how it affected my future decisions.

Forty years later, I was sitting there reliving very vividly these three conversations, and I realized what an impact a man of God could have in a young person's life. Most of these men were at the age of being grandparents. In my talk I told them how powerful the right words at the right time could be. I reminded them that they had young men and women in their congregation who were starving for a man to care about them.

I went on to say, "If you would just come up to them once or twice a week and put your arm around them, that really matters. Just pick out one or two. Ask God who needs help and some special attention. Ask them how they are doing, and just talk to them. Take a young man hunting or fishing to affirm them. Don't be afraid to tell them that to be a man of God, you don't have to have sex. That a real man of character would not do that to a girl. That sex is a gift from God to be enjoyed in marriage; otherwise, the effects can be devastating. They may not have anyone else in their lives to tell them what a man of character is like and what he would do. I put a challenge out there for them to do just that. And when you hear that someone has fallen, and someone is having a problem, that you can be someone who can speak something affirming. That you might save that infant's life. That you might save them. That you might encourage them to be the best mom or dad they can be."

86

It was like coming full circle for me. It was really a hard speaking engagement. There was a lot of emotion, but I knew how important it was for me to tell them about my experience. I told them how I sat there and cried when God told me what he wanted me to do. So, I had to share with these men what was in my heart because I knew that they could make a difference in some young person's life.

I went on to say, "You can ignore it, or you can complain to your wife that another kid's pregnant, or you can put your arm around that girl who might need a father figure and tell her that it's going to be okay. You might give her the boldness to walk away from a bad relationship and to do what she needs to do. You might need to tell a young man that he can keep himself until marriage, and that he could have a very awesome relationship because virginity and abstinence are not discussed in a lot of homes."

It was really powerful because the entire church became great supporters of us. The men came to build shelves, and they bought my storage building. Other churches and groups have come on board since. We can all be a part of the solution. We have girls here, who, if they're having a problem at home or something's going on, have plugged in and have really grabbed onto the center as a safety net. They know that if they're falling apart, they can come here and say, "Can we talk?"

We have lots of people in this community with lots of wisdom. Each of us just needs to ask what can be done to make the world better. Each of us should ask God, "Who can I disciple?" God will put people in our paths. Then these kids can grow up and have a successful family life and have a ministry and do something thirty or forty years from now and have a story that is similar to those of us who have gone on to use our painful experiences in the past to comfort others.

Questions to Consider

(1) Why did Linda feel reluctant about talking to a Christian men's group about her experiences as a young women in particular and the pregnancy center in general?

(2) What did she decide to tell them?

(3) What impact can a Godly man have in a young person's life?

(4) What did Linda mean that the experience of talking to the Christian men's group was like "coming full circle"?

(5) What did the men's group do to help the pregnancy center after her first talk?

Chapter 17

Post Abortion Recovery

I was still in the Catholic church after I got married, and we became part of the charismatic renewal. We loved the folk masses in the late seventies and early eighties in Phoenix. There were prayer meetings, and there were miracles. We loved being a part of that.

At a Frances McNutt healing seminar, the leaders announced that they would be available the next morning for people who wanted to do confession, prayer, and deal with memories that had been tormenting them. I went in and dealt with the abortion issue.

Part of what they did with inner healing was visualization. Once I started talking about it, these images that had been suppressed for many years started surfacing. He would just ask us, "What are you seeing? Let's deal with it." And they brought everything to the cross. I said that I had asked for forgiveness. Of course, the big question was—"Have you forgiven yourself?" I don't know why that is always the last thing we think of. That was the area I had to deal with that day.

The images were very real as I was seeing the process and going through forgiving the people involved. Forgiving myself. At one point he looked up at me and asked the question, "Where is Jesus in this?" He even used this visualization with victims of abuse. We always want to know when something horrible happens, "Where is Jesus? Where is

God?" I scanned the room, and over at the door in the corner, Jesus was standing there. The leader saw my reaction and knew I saw Jesus. Then he asked me what He was doing. I looked at Jesus and tears were running down His face. The leader asked, "Did you call on His name? Did you ask Him to come?" We are just like Adam and Eve. We want to hide when we are in sin. We don't call on Him to come in the midst of our sin. In my visualization, the abortion was over. Everyone had left the room, except Jesus. He said He would never leave us or forsake us. I heard Him say, "I'm still here." I saw Him go over where the baby was in a basin on the counter, pick it up, wrap it up, turn around and walk away.

It was very healing. As we prayed and went through these memories, we saw how when we put things in God's perspective and we add God's perspective to our memories, God can change them and us. It's not a scar that's unbearable anymore. Later on, I told my older children that someday when they get to Glory, and someone that you don't know comes up to you and says that he's your brother or she's your sister, you'll know who it is. Then I asked them to forgive me because that was their brother or sister that was taken from them.

Then as I got ready to do this ministry, I knew that post abortion recovery was really a part I wanted to include. Then I had to ask my local church to forgive me because I had friends who did not know about the abortion. They would end up knowing because my testimony had to go out. I've given my testimony to several women's groups in this town, and that one men's group, and almost always there is someone who comes forth and contacts me within a week or so who has had an abortion and needs someone with whom to talk. It's amazing. As the Bible tells us, we do comfort with the comfort we have received when we allow Jesus to come into our lives to heal our pain. When we go forward to help others, we discover that our suffering has not been in vain. In Romans 8:28, we find this assurance. "And we know that in all things God works for the good of those who love him, who have been called according to his purpose." Often, our most effective ministry will come out of our deepest hurts.[2]

Questions to Consider

(1) What did Linda mean that she took her guilt about having an abortion to the cross?

(2) Why was this important in her healing process?

(3) Why did Linda feel that she had to ask her children and her church for forgiveness?

(4) How has being honest about her experience helped other people?

(5) What does the following quotation mean? Explain.

"Your most effective ministry will come out of your deepest hurts."

(6) Do you have to be a minister in a church to have a ministry of your own? Why or why not?

(7) Do you have to be an adult or older person to have a ministry?

Part 3
Going Deeper

(1) Have you ever acted in the role of an enabler? Explain.

(2) Has the lack of communication with your father or any other family member impacted your life? Explain.

(3) Have you ever felt that you were keeping "peace at any cost"? What did it cost you?

(4) Can it be destructive if taken too far? Explain.

(5) Have events shaped your life in ways you didn't understand at the time? Explain.

(6) Has a Godly man or woman had an impact in your life?

(7) Is there something you need to take to the cross?

(8) Do you need help getting there?

Responding to Scripture

How do the following scriptures apply to you and your life? Explain.

Do not let your hearts be troubled. Trust in God; trust also in me. (John 14:1)

For God did not give us a spirit of timidity, but a spirit of power, of love and self-discipline. (1Timothy 1:7).

And we know that in all things God works for the good of those who love him, who have been called according to his purpose. (Romans 8:28)

For God so loved the world that he gave his one and only son that who ever believes in him shall not perish but have eternal life. (John 3:16)

But the fruit of the Spirit is love, joy, peace, patience, kindness, goodness, faithfulness, gentleness and self-control. Against such things there is no law. (Galatians 5:22-23)

Do you look for the "fruits of the Holy Spirit" in a man you date or plan to marry? Do you work on developing the "fruits of the Holy Spirit" in yourself? Why do all humans need a relationship with Christ and the help of the Holy Spirit to work on the "fruits of the Holy Spirit"? Will we ever attain all of these fruits every day for the rest of our lives on this earth? Why or why not?

May the God of hope fill you with all joy and peace as you trust in him, so that you may overflow with hope by the power of the Holy Spirit. (Romans 15:13)

Part Four
Moving Forward God's Way

by

Dr. Wayne Shaw

Chapter 18

Looking Back

S everal years ago, I attended a Promise Keepers rally that was geared to challenging us to be better fathers. One of the exercises that day was to rate our own fathers on a scale of 1-10, with 10 being the best. I gave my father an average rating. He wasn't too bad, but he had his faults. Then they had us get into small groups to discuss our fathers and why we had given them the rating we had. In my group were two other men, an older man and a younger man. If my memory serves me correctly, the older man gave his dad a 1. The younger man gave his dad a 0. I sat there astonished as I listened to their stories. Tears rolled down the cheeks of the older man as he told how he and his father had been alienated. I don't remember his reason, but I remember his pain. He told how he would go to his father's grave site and weep and pray because he so desperately would like to have been reconciled to his father before he died. The younger man, with almost no emotion, told how his father had tied him up like a dog and beat him with a belt.

I sat there thinking, in light of what I had just heard, my father deserved a 10. He worked hard and always provided for his family. He made us work hard, but that taught us a good work ethic. We never worried about going hungry. We never worried that our father might not return home, that he might just disappear. That thought never entered our minds. I thought he was too strict, probably those who knew me thought he was not strict enough. He never abused us. He seldom told us that he loved us, but we knew he did. He definitely had a great deal of influence on my life. Today, I am a minister because of his example and encouragement.

Recently, I was with the leadership of our church in a retreat setting, and I had them construct their timeline consisting of the major events and people who had impacted their lives. They were to put a yellow sticky tab for each positive event or person and a red one for each negative one. Then we went around the room, each telling his story. Some had mostly yellow sticky tabs. Others had more red than yellow. I watched and listened as some of these grown men wept while they told their story, a story of a painful past. The one thing that struck me was how much our parents impact who we are. Generally, it was the father whose impact made a longer lasting impression, either positively or negatively.

I know that none of us as earthly fathers are perfect. We all have our weaknesses. What I have found interesting is that there were things my parents did, that I said I would never do. But then, when I least expected it, I found myself doing the very thing I said I would not. Old habits are hard to break. We follow examples much closer than we do lectures.

Since I had a good father, I am amazed how many fathers don't even attempt to love and care for their own children, but rather are absent, abusive, or neglectful. It seems so unnatural. If your father was abusive or absent, let me say that you did not deserve that. It was not your fault. You were the victim. Don't blame yourself. You may suffer shame for that but never feel guilty for something over which you had no control.

Questions to Consider

(1) Why do you think Dr. Shaw changed his opinion about his father after the Promise Keepers rally?

(2) What does the following statement mean?

"We follow examples much closer than we do lectures."

(3) Are you responsible for the actions of other people toward you?

Chapter 19

Shame, Guilt, and Forgiveness

Let me take a moment to explain the difference between shame and guilt. Guilt occurs when you have done something that is wrong, broken the law, or committed an offense. When you do wrong, you should feel guilty because you have violated your conscience. In childhood your parents told you what was right or wrong. As you grew older, you understood that the law had boundaries you were not to cross.

As a Christian, you know that God has a standard, and when you disobey, you are guilty. As you come to know and love God, you learn that if you want the best out of life, you should try to live up to the standards He has set for you. Someone has accurately said that we don't break God's laws, they break us. A great deal of the pain and hardship you suffer comes from doing it your way and not God's way.

I would define shame as the feeling that you are wrong because of what someone else has done to you. You feel guilty, for lack of a better word, because of someone else's action. You may feel dirty and unworthy because someone abused you. No matter how often others tell you not to feel guilty or shameful, it still may take a long time to erase the pain and hurt.

The sad truth is that you cannot change the past. No matter how hard you try, you cannot, but you must put it behind you. That is not easy. It is often a very painful journey. You need to see your father as a human being. Though he may have been weak or misguided or simply mean, he was human. My guess is if you had gotten to know him better, you would have found a great deal of pain in his past. That does not excuse what he did to you or what he did not do for you, but it does help explain. The truth of the matter is that in the midst of our pain it is very, very difficult to attempt to understand the pain of the other person. It is a sad but true commentary, most abusers have been abused. "Men experience father hunger just as much as women—perhaps even more. And having been provided such poor role models, they themselves often find it difficult to respond in a loving way."[1] You must stop the cycle.

After that difficult step, you will have to take one that is even harder. You will need to forgive him. You may say that he does not deserve it. And you are right. You may ask how you can forgive him when he has not changed and will not change. In that case, he does not and will never deserve it. But let me remind you, forgiveness is never deserved. If it were deserved, we would not need it. Forgiveness is available only to the undeserving.

When you forgive someone for what they have done to you and they refuse to change, you might have to stay away from them to be safe. Even if they do change, you still might find it difficult to have any kind of relationship with them. Forgiveness doesn't always signal the start of a new and vigorous relationship. The other party has to be truly sorry for what he has done, and both parties must desire a renewed relationship. No matter what happens as a result, you will still need to forgive him for your own sake. The anger, the bitterness, and the hurt that you carry around is not hurting him, but you. You must let go of it. Bitterness in your heart is like your taking a cyanide pill and hoping **he** will die.

In *What's So Amazing About Grace*, author Phillip Yancey tells of hearing an immigrant rabbi make an astonishing statement: "Before coming to America, I had to forgive Adolf Hitler. I did not want to bring Hitler inside me to my new country."[2] Lewis Smedes, also a well-known Christian author, helps us understand why we need to forgive. He points out, "the first and often the only person to be helped by forgiveness is the person who does the forgiveness. When we genuinely forgive, we set a prisoner free and then discover that the prisoner we set free was us."[3]

Questions to Consider

(1) What is the difference between shame and guilt? Explain.

(2) What does the following statement mean:

"In the midst of our own pain, it is very, very difficult to attempt to understand the pain of the other person."

(3) Why is it important to forgive someone, even if they refuse to change?

(4) Does forgiving someone mean that you approve of their behavior?

(5) Does forgiving someone mean that you have to have a relationship with them if it is physically or emotionally damaging?

(6) What does the following statement mean?

"The first and often the only person to be helped by forgiveness is the person who does the forgiveness. When we genuinely forgive, we set a prisoner free and then discover that the prisoner we set free was us."

Chapter 20

Moving Forward God's Way

The most important step you can take, the most helpful step you can take is to let God, your heavenly Father, truly be you father. God wants to be father to the fatherless. This will be hard because your views of your heavenly Father has been distorted by the behavior of your earthly father.

Over the years I have had ties with Cookson Hills Christian Ministries. My parents worked there in the early 70's. Our church has helped put children there who needed a safe place in which to grow. But one of the saddest notes of this ministry is that they cannot talk to the children about God as our father, because many of these, like some of you, have been abused or neglected by their own father, and to mention that God is our father gives them a very distorted view of God. Our view of our earthly father greatly impacts our view of our heavenly Father.

Not only does our father impact our view of God for good or bad, our father also has some effect on who we choose to marry. Why are we so slow to recognize the fact that we are prone to marry someone like our father? Why would someone who had an alcoholic parent marry an alcoholic? Why would someone who has been abused marry an abusive man? Why would they not want to break the cycle? Why would they not want something different? I have listened to and read some authorities on that subject. I still don't comprehend it. I guess the bottom line is that we tend to marry someone like the only model with whom we are familiar.

Did you hear about the lady who married Mr. Right? She just did not know that his first name was Always. Take time to find a good mate. Investigate the person thoroughly. Don't use your own dad as a standard, use your heavenly Father. I know that you are not going to find someone who is perfect, but do find someone who loves God and is growing in their faith. Someone who treats you like a lady. Someone who gives you value. Someone who sees potential in you. Someone who puts your needs first.

Marriage can be wonderful. I have been married for forty-three years and cannot imagine life without my wife Anna. She has been supportive, encouraging, loving, trustworthy, and helpful. She did a great job as a loving mother of our three children and caring for twenty foster children over the years. She still laughs at my jokes. She is indeed a virtuous woman, a gift from God.

Someone has said that marriage is like flies on a screen door on a hot July day. Those on the outside want in and those on the inside want out. A good marriage can be a taste of heaven on earth. A bad marriage can be a taste of hell. Take your time and make a wise choice. Look for red flags before marriage. It is better not to be married than to marry the wrong person. One of my mother's favorite sayings was; "Marry in haste, repent in leisure."

Sex is also a gift from God. It can be beautiful and fulfilling, or it can be devastating and filled with deep regret and remorse. God designed sex to be in the context of a monogamous marriage relationship between a man and a woman. Where there is love and commitment, there will be joy and fulfillment. Each partner should seek to fulfill the needs of the other. Contrary to popular opinion and what you see on television, research has repeatedly shown that partners who are married to each other have a greater satisfaction, enjoyment, and fulfillment in sex than their unmarried counterparts.

Outside of that context, there is a lack of commitment to the other person. Commitment brings a sense of security. I hear people say that a marriage license is only a piece of paper. What a stupid argument! If that's all it is, then it is not a marriage. Let us reframe that picture for just a moment. You get stopped by a police officer and he says, "May I see your license, registration, and proof of insurance?" You respond, "I don't bother with that; those are just pieces of paper." (I dare you to try it!)

Outside of marriage, the purpose is often to satisfy selfish desire and use the other person. Women give sex to get love. Men give love to get sex. Sometimes that is true in marriage as well, but true love seeks what is best for the other person. That is another reason why it is important to take your time before getting married. You need to check the maturity level of the individual, their commitment, their values, their goals in life, and their willingness to put you first.

In our society abortion has become a quick fix for an unwanted pregnancy. In her story Linda has so eloquently told you about the pain that does not go away until God heals us. One summer, a few years ago, we did a series of sermons called Hot Topics. One of those hot topics was abortion. I will not preach you the sermon, but I will say I am unashamedly prolife. I believe that God is the giver of life. But as I came to the end of the sermon, I asked, "What would Jesus say to the person who had an abortion?" Here is what I think Jesus would say and do. He would kneel before you, take your hands in His nail scarred hands and say, "Do you see those scars on my hands? I died for your sins. If you will simply come to me and be my child, you can have your sins forgiven. As you walk with me, I will also begin to heal your heart and your hurt. As for your unborn child, I know you miss him/her. There is an emptiness in your heart. But you need to know that he/she is safe in My Father's hands. If you will follow me, one day you can be with that child for all eternity in a place of joy and peace."

Questions to Consider

(1) How can your view of your earthly father distort your view of your heavenly Father?

(2) What characteristics should you look for in a man you choose to marry?

(3) Is being a Godly man high on your list? Should it be?

(4) How is sex a gift from God?

(5) How does God want this gift to be used?

(6) How do men and women view sex differently? Explain.

(7) Even though God hates abortion, can He forgive someone who has had one?

Chapter 21

God's Healing Hand

In the first section of the book, Judith talks about how much the story of the sinful woman meant to her. From it she learned to accept the love, grace, and forgiveness that Christ freely offers when we are able to open our hearts to receive it. Most people can relate to this story in some way. In my ministry, I have seen the impact this story has made on the lives of many. I am going to refer to it again because it has layers and layers of meaning and demonstrates the love of Jesus in so many different ways.

When we do wrong, too often those closest to us heap guilt on us instead of grace. They are quick to tell us what we have done wrong. They make us feel guilty, but they are not as quick to help us get our lives straightened out. In John 8, Jesus was teaching in the temple area when the religious leaders of that day brought before him a woman who had been caught in "the very act of adultery." They did not care about the morals of Jerusalem; they wanted to entrap Jesus. "The law of Moses says stone her, what do you say?" They thought they had caught Jesus on the horns of a dilemma. If He said, "No, don't stone her," they would accuse Him of not keeping the Law of Moses. If He said, "Yes, stone her," then they would accuse Him of going against Roman law, which the Jews were under at that time.

There is more evidence of their hypocrisy. They brought the woman caught in the act of adultery. Doesn't it take two to tango? Where was the man? Wasn't he guilty too? Too often in our society, there is a double standard. Since the woman is the one who gets pregnant, she is the one who bears the brunt of the humiliation.

As they were accusing this woman, Jesus stooped down and began writing in the sand with his finger. We have no idea what he wrote. They kept pressing the matter, so he straightened up and said to them, "If any one of you is without sin, let him be the first to throw a stone at her." Then returned to His writing on the ground.

One by one, they began to leave, the oldest ones first. In that day when a stoning occurred, the oldest were to throw the first stones. After they left, Jesus stood up and asked, "Woman, where are they?" Has no one condemned you?"

"No one, sir," she said.

"Then neither do I condemn you," Jesus declared. "Go now and leave your life of sin."

What a statement of grace, "neither do I condemn you." He was the only one there who was without sin, so He could have cast the first stone, yet instead of guilt and condemnation, He offered grace and forgiveness.

Jesus forgives our past, but he also gives us hope for the future. "Go now and leave your life of sin." He gives us hope because He not only calls us from our life of sin, He calls us to a new life in Him. Leaving the past behind us involves not only finding forgiveness, but leaving our past lifestyle and enjoying a relationship with the Jesus Christ who forgives and offers to us eternal life.

While Jesus died for our sins and willingly forgives us, He is definitely not saying that it is now all right for us to go on sinning. For Jesus to forgive our sins does not mean He is condoning our sins anymore than forgiving your father or whoever else may have abused you condones what he did or does it endorse their doing it again. It simply means that the debt from the past has been cancelled.[3]

True healing, healing of the heart, healing of those deep wounds of the past comes from God. I count it a privilege to know the four ladies in this book, actually five, my wife Anna, director of the Christian H.E.L.P. Center, who was mentioned in Linda's story. I have worked with each of these women in various capacities as they serve God. The only thing I find more astonishing than their stories is the healing that has taken place in their hearts and their lives. I am amazed at how God's grace has healed them after all they have been through and how God is using them now. God has gifted them to sense who is going through a difficult time and reach out to them and bring God's grace and love to their lives. The Bible says, "Praise be to the God and Father of our Lord Jesus Christ, the Father of compassion and the God of all comfort, who comforts us in all our troubles, so that we can comfort those in any trouble with the comfort we ourselves have received from God." (2 Cor. 1:3-4) Part of your healing is going to be helping others who have gone down the same rough roads you have and helping them to find love and hope. Because of your experiences, though they may have been very painful, you too can be a blessing to someone else who is suffering.

My daughter had a propensity for bringing home strays, especially dogs and cats. This made her mother and I worry about what stray she might bring home and say, "This is the guy I want to marry." In her senior year of high school, she asked if a classmate of hers could come and live with us. This girl was being kicked out of her home. I think she knew before she asked what the answer would be, for she often had to share her room with a foster child who came to live with us for a while.

We got her friend back in school, and she graduated with our daughter. There were two things I remember about this young lady. First, because of her past, she could not sit still. She had to be doing something. She could not stand time alone, quiet time alone. Perhaps, if she kept busy, she didn't have time to deal with her emotional pain.

Secondly, she had very low self-worth. The treatment she had received in her past greatly damaged her self-image. Because of what had been done to her, she could not see herself as important. Probably the cruelest thing I did to her was have her sit down one day and write me a list of twelve things she liked about herself. In retrospect, I think it was borderline torture. She was a pretty girl. She was an intelligent girl. She was an energetic girl. She had trouble loving herself because her father had not loved her. She did not see herself as important or valuable because her parents had not.

As you begin to heal, you will need to heal from the inside out. You need a healing of the heart. In many different ways, all the ladies in the stories and I have told you the same thing. You need to come to the cross of Christ, but you need someone who will help you get there. Someone who cares. Someone who understands. My good friend Shirley Hasson shared with me something profound she had written in her Bible. "Friends may ease the pain and hurt, but only God can cleanse and heal the wound."

In his book, *The Search for Significance*, Robert McGee shares this insight. "Those who have received poor parental modeling need new models—loving Christian friends to experience the love and grace of God. Through his body of believers, God often provides us with models of His love, so that our perceptions of His character can be slowly reshaped into one that is more accurate, resulting in a healthier relationship with Him. Then our deep emotional, spiritual, and relational wounds can begin to heal, and we can more fully experience God's unconditional love."[4]

You are valuable. You are created in the image of God. You are important, so important that the Son of God died for you. You are loved. Jesus Christ loves you so much that He gave His life for you.

In Jeremiah 29:11, our heavenly Father promises us: "For I know the plans I have for you," declares the Lord, "plans to prosper you and not to harm you, plans to give you hope and a future." Life is a journey that should not be taken alone. Let your heavenly Father walk with you. Let God touch you with His healing hand.

And Then He Touched Me
by
Judith David

I play a child's game.
No one wants me on their side.
Don't want to feel pain.
Anger hardens into pride.

And then He touched me.
Saw tears streaming down my face.
Reached down and touched me.
With His love and gentle grace,
He reached down from up above,
Wrapped me in a blanket of His love.
I'm glad He touched me.

Don't say the right words.
Always trying to fit in.
Don't wear the right clothes.
I'm dying to be thin.

And then He touched me.
Who flung the stars and shaped the land
Reached down and touched me.
He loves me just the way I am.
He reached down from up above,
Wrapped me in a blanket of his love.
So glad He touched me.

The Great Jehovah,
The God Almighty, King of Kings
Reached down and touched me.
Now He's my life; He's everything.
He's forgiven all my sins.
Someday I'm going home with Him.
Thank God He touched me.

Questions to Consider

(1) Is there a double standard in our society when a woman gets pregnant? Explain.

(2) After Jesus forgives the woman caught in the act of adultery, does He condemn her?

(3) What does He expect her to do after He forgives her?

(4) How does Christ's forgiveness give us hope for the future?

(5) How can helping others be a part of your own healing?

(6) Why did the girl Dr. Shaw's daughter brought home to live with her family have so much trouble saying something good about herself?

(7) Why did she not see herself as important?

(8) Was this young girl important in God's eyes?

(9) Do you think the ladies in this book experienced healing from telling their stories to help others? Why or why not?

(10) Explain the following statement:

"Friends may ease the pain and hurt, but only God can cleanse and heal the wound."

(11) How can people who have received poor parenting learn to experience the love of God?

(12) How can being a child of God give you a new identity and feeling of self-worth?

Part 4
Going Deeper

(1) Do you have someone you need to forgive?

(2) Does this mean that you have to continue to have a relationship with them?

(3) Who does forgiveness help the most?

(4) How does the following statement apply to your life?

"Bitterness in your heart is like your taking a cyanide pill and hoping **he** (your father) will die."

(5) Do you want to be a child of God and receive a new identity through Christ?

(6) How can you know that God is present in your life? Name some instances in which you felt that God acted in the role of your Father. Name some instances in which He guided you or protected you.

(7) How can you get to know the heavenly Father in a more personal way?

(8) How can you use other Christians to show you God's love?

(9) How do you start the process of letting your heavenly Father walk through the journey of life with you?

Responding to Scripture:

How do the following scriptures apply to you and your life? Explain.

Not only so, but we also rejoice in our sufferings, because we know that suffering produces perseverance; perseverance, character; and character, hope. And hope does not disappoint us, because God has poured out his love into our hearts by the Holy Spirit, whom he has given us. (Romans 5:3-5)

Praise be to the God and Father of our Lord Jesus Christ, the Father of compassion and the God of all comfort, who comforts us in all our troubles, so that we can comfort those in any trouble with the comfort we ourselves have received from God. (2 Corinthians 1:37)

For all have sinned, and come short of the glory of God. (Romans 3:23)

For the wages of sin is death, but the gift of God is eternal life through Jesus Christ our Lord. (Romans 6:23)

For if you forgive men when they sin against you, your heavenly Father will also forgive you. But if you do not forgive men their sins, your father will not forgive your sins. (Matthew 6:14)

For whosoever shall call upon the name of the lord shall be saved. (Romans 10:13)

"For I know the plans I have for you," declares the Lord, "plans to prosper you and not to harm you, plans to give you hope and a future." (Jeremiah 29:11)

No eyes have seen,
 no ear has heard,
no mind has conceived
 what God has prepared
for those who love him.   (1 Corinthians 2)

Suggested Reading List

Beattie, Melody. *Codependent No More: How to Stop Controlling Others and Start Caring For Yourself.* **Center City, Minnesota: Hazelden, 1992.**

"A simple, straightforward, readable map of the perplexing world of codependency—charting the path to freedom and a lifetime of healing, hope, and happiness." (back cover)

Dobson, Dr. James. *When God Doesn't Make Sense.* **Wheaton, Illinois, Tyndale House Publishers, 1993.**

"An immensely practical book for those who are struggling with trials and heartaches they can't understand." (back cover)

Hemfelt, Robert, Minrinth, Frank, and Meier, Paul. *Love Is a Choice.* **Nashville, Tennessee: Thomas Nelson Publishers, 1989.**

"A definitive book on letting go of unhealthy relationships." (front cover)
These three experienced doctors explain codependency, dysfunctional family dynamics, steps to recovery, and letting God's unconditional love meet your "deepest emotional needs and your hunger for love." (back cover)

McGee, Robert S. *Father Hunger.* Ann Arbor, Michigan: Servant Publications, 1993.

Father Hunger describes "the emptiness that many of us experience because we still crave the comfort and security that our fathers did not provide." (back cover)

McGee, Robert S. *The Search for Significance.* Nashville, Tennessee: Word Publishing, 1998.

"Seeing your true worth though God's eyes." (front cover)

McGee, Robert S. *The Search for Significance: Student Edition.* Nashville, Tennessee: W Publishing Group, 2003.

"You'll discover the lies you have believed about who you are—lies that may be robbing you of experiencing real happiness. You will also learn how to test your fear of rejection and learn how to overcome the issues you struggle with most often. This is your chance to change everything by changing the way you think." (back cover.)

Meyer, Joyce. *Seven Things That Steal Your Joy: Overcoming the Obstacles to Your Happiness.* New York: Warner Faith, 2004.

"Through inspiring passages from Scripture and words of wisdom mined from her ministry and her own experiences, she shows you how to find joy and keep it." (front flap)

Norwood, Robin. *Women Who Love Too Much: When You Keep Wishing and Hoping He'll Change.* **New York: Pocket Books, 1985.**

A must read for women who keep getting stuck in obsessive relationships.

Smedes, Lewis B. *Healing the Hurts We Don't Deserve.* **New York: Pocket Books, 1984.**

"Lewis B. Smedes shows you how to move from hurting and hating to healing and reconciliation. With the lessons of forgiveness, you can establish healthier relationships, reclaim the happiness that should be yours, and achieve lasting peace of mind." (back cover)

Smedes, Lewis B. *The Art of Forgiving: When We Need to Forgive and Don't Know How.* **New York: Ballantine Books, 1996.**

"If you are ready to make peace with those who have hurt or betrayed you, there can be no finer road map than this book. Lewis B. Smedes brings true forgiveness, 'God's own gift,' within the capacity of every wounded person, even in circumstances when only hate and vengefulness seem possible." (back cover)

Stoop, David. *Making Peace With Your Father.* **Wheaton, Illinois: Tyndale House Publishers, 1992.**

"When you were little he was the most important man in your life. Now that you're grown up, he still affects everything you are and do—sometimes in ways you don't suspect. It's time to heal childhood hurts and affirm the strong bond between you.

It's time to make peace with your father, with yourself, and with God." (front cover)

Warren, Rick. *The Purpose Driven life.* **Grand Rapids, Michigan: Zondervan, 2002.**

This book will "help you understand why you are alive and reveal God's amazing plan for you—both here and now, and for eternity." (back cover)

Notes

Introduction:
Before You Give Your Heart Away

[1]Dr. Robert Hemfelt, Dr. Frank Minrinth and Dr. Paul Meier, *Love Is a Choice* (Nashville, Tennessee: Thomas Nelson Publishers, 1989), 28.

Part One: Earthly Father/Heavenly Father

[1]Rick Warren, *The Purpose Driven Life* (Grand Rapids, Michigan: Zondervan, 2002), 127.

[2]Jim Craddock, *A.W.O.L. Parents* (Oklahoma City, Oklahoma: GTN Publishing, 2007), 10.

[3]David Stoop, *Making Peace With Your Father* (Wheaton, Illinois: Tyndale House Publishers, 1992), 126.

[4]Robert S. McGee, *Father Hunger* (Ann Arbor, Michigan: Servant Publications, 1993), 68.

[5]Stoop, front cover.

[6]McGee, *Father Hunger,* 10.

[7]McGee, *Father Hunger,* 37.

[8]McGee, *Father Hunger,* 18.

[9]RobertMcGee, *The Search for Significance* (Nashville, Tennessee: Word Publishing, 1998), 28.

[10]Warren, 85.

[11]Tim Sledge, *Making Peace With Your Past: Help for Adult Children of Dysfunctional Families* (Nashville, Tennessee: LifeWay Press, 1992), 22.

[12]Warren, 111.

[13]Oprah Winfrey, "The Oprah Winfrey Show," Chicago, Illinois, Harpo Productions, 5 Oct. 2007.

[14]Sledge, 32.

[15]McGee, *The Search for Significance,* 2.

[16]McGee, *The Search for Significance*, 3.

[17]McGee, *The Search for Significance*, 7.

[18]Margery Williams, Illustrated by William Nicholson, *The Velveteen Rabbit* (New York: HarperCollins, 1975), 12 & 13.

Part Two: Hiding the Shame

[1]Sledge, 13.

[2]Sledge, 46.

[3]Sledge, 52-53.

[4]McGee*, Father Hunger*, 122.

[5]McGee, *The Search for Significance*, 4.

[6]McGee, *The Search for Significance*, 12.

[7]Hemfelt, Minrinth, and Meier, *7.*

[8]Craddock, 9.

[9]Craddock, 10.

[10]Louann Brizendine, M.D., *The Female Brain* (New York: Broadway Books, 2006), 91.

[11]Warren, 28.

Part Three: Coming Full Circle

[1]Hemfelt, Minrinth and Meier, 58.

[2]Warren, 275.

Part Four: Moving Forward God's Way

[1]McGee, *Father Hunger*, 19.

[2]Phillip Yancey, *What's So Amazing About Grace?* (Grand Rapids, Michigan: Zondervan, 1998), 99-100.

[3]Lewis Smedes, *Forgive and Forget: Healing the Hurts We Don't Deserve* (New York: Pocket Books, 1984), 170.

[4]McGee, *The Search for Significance*, 82.

Works Cited

Brizendine, Louann. *The Female Brain.* New York: Broadway Books, 2006.

Craddock, Jim. *A. W. O. L. Parents.* Oklahoma City, Oklahoma: GTN Publishing, 2007.

Hemfelt, Robert, Minrinth, Frank, and Meier, Paul. *Love Is a Choice.* Nashville, Tennessee: Thomas Nelson Publishers, 1989.

McGee, Robert S. *Father Hunger.* Ann Arbor, Michigan: Servant Publications, 1993.

McGee Robert S. *The Search for Significance.* Nashville, Tennessee: Word Publishing, 1998.

Sledge, Tim. *Making Peace with Your Past: Help for Adult Children of Dysfunctional Families.* Nashville, Tennessee: LifeWay Press, 1992.

Smedes, Lewis. *Forgive and Forget: Healing the Hurts We Don't Deserve.* New York: Pocket Books, 1984.

Stoop, David. *Making Peace with Your Father.* Wheaton, Illinois: Tyndale House Publishers, 1992.

Warren, Rick. *The Purpose Driven Life.* Grand Rapids, Michigan: Zondervan, 2002.

Williams, Margery. Illustrated by William Nicholson. *The Velveteen Rabbit.* New York: HarperCollins, 1975.

Winfrey, Oprah. "The Oprah Winfrey Show." Chicago, Illinois. Harpo Productions. 5 Oct. 2007.

Yancey, Phillip. *What's So Amazing About Grace?* Grand Rapids, Michigan: Zondervan, 1998.

CPSIA information can be obtained
at www.ICGtesting.com
Printed in the USA
FFOW02n2143240615
14619FF